INTELLECTUAL PROPERTY RIGHTS

INTELLECTUAL PROPERTY RIGHTS

NEERAJ PANDEY

Associate Professor
NITIE (National Institute of Industrial Engineering)
Mumbai, Maharashtra

KHUSHDEEP DHARNI

Associate Professor
PAU (Punjab Agricultural University)
Ludhiana, Punjab

PHI Learning Private Limited

Delhi-110092
2025

In fond memory of ***Shri Asoke K. Ghosh*** *(October 1942 – February 2024), Founder Chairman and Managing Director of PHI Learning, whose vision endlessly inspires.*

The Legacy Continues....

Published by Pushpita Ghosh, PHI Learning Private Limited, Rimjhim House, 111, Patparganj Industrial Estate, Delhi-110092 and Printed by Star Print-O-Bind, F-31, Okhla Industrial Area Phase 1, New Delhi-110020.

₹495.00

INTELLECTUAL PROPERTY RIGHTS
Neeraj Pandey and Khushdeep Dharni

ISBN-978-81-203-4989-6 (Print Book)
ISBN-978-93-5443-544-7 (e-Book)

The export rights of the book are vested solely with the publisher.

To my loving son and daughter

Atharva Sheersh Pandey and Avantika Pandey

—Neeraj Pandey

To my loving sons

Keshav Dharni and Grahil Dharni

—Khushdeep Dharni

Contents

Preface

In the contemporary times, progress and well-being of humanity is largely driven by the capacity to create and innovate. For sustenance and acceleration of all-round prosperity there is a need to build and stimulate the initiatives ushering creativity. Intellectual property is purely a creation of human mind. There is hardly any sphere of life that has gone untouched by intellectual property. Global economy is rapidly transforming into knowledge economy and physical resources are being substituted with intellectual resources. Wealth creation in the modern world is primarily based on intellectual property. One of many ways to strengthen knowledge economy is recognition and treatment of knowledge as economic good. Intellectual property regulations play a key role in ensuring a mechanism for protection and fair valuation of knowledge-based output, i.e. intellectual property.

Trade Related aspects of Intellectual Property Rights (TRIPS) under World Trade Organization (WTO) provide the basic framework for the creation of intellectual property. Off late, domain of intellectual property has started catching the attention of policy makers, academicians and the business executives. This is evident from the fact that courses on intellectual property are being introduced at graduate level and post graduate level programs throughout the world.

Understanding and gaining knowledge of Intellectual Property and related regulations are important for the organizations and for every individual. Organizations can use this knowledge not only to protect their Intellectual Property lawfully, but can also avoid infringing upon intellectual property owned by others. In the modern times, intellectual property is the key to garner a sustainable competitive advantage. Structured and enforced intellectual property regulations provide an incentive to business organizations to invest aggressively in R&D and knowledge based initiatives. IP regulations are useful for the customers as well. Customers can be assured of authentic products and services with stringent IP regulations in place.

This book 'Intellectual Property Rights' has been organized into ten chapters. There is mini case let at the end of each chapter. First chapter of the book acquaints the readers with the concept of Intellectual Property, and introduces the WTO Agreement. Chapters 2 to Chapter 7 deal with various types of Intellectual Property Rights, such as Patents, Copyrights, Trade Marks, Industrial Designs, Integrated Circuits and Geographical Indications. These chapters provide in-depth and detailed insights of regulations and procedures for protection of Intellectual Property Rights. Chapter 8 deals with the creation of Intellectual Property and spells out the conceptual framework for creativity and innovation. Management of Intellectual Property is as important as its creation. Chapter 9 describes the activities for management and commercialization of Intellectual Property Rights. Chapter 10 highlights the emerging issues in Intellectual Property Rights. To give a practical insight on what is happening in the fields of Intellectual Property Rights globally, two real-life cases have been added separately at the end of the book.

Domain of Intellectual Property has many facets ranging from creation and acquisition to protection and commercialization. There is a need to get a holistic view of IP domain because one weak link in the chain can lead to sub-optimization of the entire value chain. Given the diversity of IP activities and interdisciplinary nature, it's an uphill task to produce a comprehensive yet concise piece of work on the subject. Another challenge while writing a book on a subject with lots of law content is to strike a balance between complex legal terms and lucid language.

We hope to come up to the expectations of the readers on these issues. Present text is an effort to assimilate the vast domain of Intellectual Property in a size that is intelligible to the readers.

NEERAJ PANDEY
KHUSHDEEP DHARNI

Acknowledgements

There are many persons who motivated and provided support to write this book. Firstly we are thankful to our students and colleagues at our respective institutions viz. Thapar University, Patiala (where initially both the authors were Faculty); NITIE Mumbai; Johns Hopkins University, USA and Punjab Agricultural University, Ludhiana; who enthused us to write a lucid and concise book on Intellectual Property Rights. We thank the entire publication team at PHI for their consistent support. Special thanks are due to Pushpita Ghosh, Director PHI; Malaya R. Parida, Manager—Acquisitions; Ruchira Dash; Babita Misra and Lakshmi from PHI for their support during the entire publication process.

NEERAJ PANDEY
KHUSHDEEP DHARNI

I want to heartily thank my parents Shri Daya Shankar Pandey and Smt. Renuka Pandey for their eternal blessings and guidance. I am grateful to my brothers Shri Anil Kumar Pandey, Shri Sunil Pandey, Shri Sanjay Pandey and my sister Prof. Anita Ojha who are always there for me. I want to thank my wife, Chitra Pandey for her unconditional support.

I express my sincere gratitude to Prof. Karuna Jain, Director NITIE for extending her full support whenever required.

NEERAJ PANDEY

I bow to Pujya Gurudev Swami Vidyanand Ji Maharaj for seeking blessings and lifelong patronage. I am really thankful to my mother, Smt. Raksha Bhambi, for her affection and care. Words are inadequate to express the love and support I got from my wife Dr. Sonika Sharma.

KHUSHDEEP DHARNI

CHAPTER 1

Introduction to Intellectual Property and World Trade Organization

The word *Intellectual Property* may sound alien to someone's ears. But when we pick any product/services around us from the routines of our life it forms as part of an intellectual property. Take example of a cell phone from Nokia, first look may describe it as something common without anything special. More attention to a simple cell phone will reveal that it is compiled but of numerous intellectual property rights, starting from trade mark to the patents and layout designs of integrated circuits. While watching TV, we do not realize the fact that the process involves so many combinations of copyright, broadcasting and patents on transmission of signals. Similarly, in our day-to-day lives, we ignore the world around that is full of products and services based on intellectual property. A lot of effort and investment goes in creating these intellectual property rights, embedding these into products and services, and in getting the monetary returns back.

1.1 INTELLECTUAL PROPERTY—DEFINITION

World Intellectual Property Organization (WIPO) defines Intellectual Property (IP) as the creations of the mind: inventions, literary and artistic works, and symbols, names, images, and designs, used in commerce.

1.1.1 Intellectual Property vs. Physical Property

Property can be broadly categorized into physical property and intellectual property. There are a number of basis on which physical property can be differentiated from intellectual property. Physical property exists in the physical shape, and is tangible, whereas intellectual property is intangible in nature. Intellectual property is purely creation of human mind while physical property will invariably include physical resources, such as metals, construction material etc. that have physical existence. Further, physical property can be both private and public in nature. But intellectual property is essentially private in nature, i.e. belongs either to a natural person or legal person (companies, institutions). Physical property may be available in limited quantity worldwide, but no such limitation exists on intellectual property as it can be created without any end.

There are a number of similarities between physical and intellectual property as well. Like physical properties such as buildings, automobiles, etc., intellectual property can be owned, bought and sold, rented, protected and infringed upon by the others. Right of exclusivity available on the physical property (excluding/refraining others from the use of property) is also available on intellectual property and legal remedies, and damages can be claimed in case of infringements.

1.1.2 Importance of Intellectual Property

Intellectual property is assuming a greater importance with the rise of the knowledge economy. Since agreement on Trade Related aspects of Intellectual Property Rights (TRIPS) under World Trade Organization (WTO) intellectual property has started catching the fancy of the policy makers, academicians and the business executives. A few salient points highlighting the importance of intellectual property are cited as follows:

- Exclusive right on the use of IP is the biggest motivation behind creation of intellectual property. Inventors and artists are encouraged to go for creative pursuits, only because ultimately exclusive rights are available on the newly created IP. Creators can use these exclusive rights for getting financial incentives and carry on their creative pursuits further.
- Intellectual property is the primary means of wealth creation in the society. Goods and services created through intellectual property add on to the wealth of the inventors and entrepreneurs, benefitting the whole society in the process.
- Customers are able to enjoy improved goods and services, and are exposed to fabulous artistic and literary works on account of creation of IP.
- Business organizations are able to profit through increased revenue generation and creation of entry barriers on account of exclusive manufacturing and marketing rights provided by intellectual property.
- IP can also lead to cost saving for the society through better production methods and save limited natural and physical resources from being depleted fast.

Classification of property has been presented in Figure 1.1. According to WIPO, intellectual property can be divided into two categories, namely industrial property and copyright. Industrial property includes patents, trade marks, industrial designs and geographical indications. Copyright is awarded for the literary and artistic work, and covers works, such as novels, poems, plays, films, music, drawings, paintings, photographs, sculptures and architectural designs.

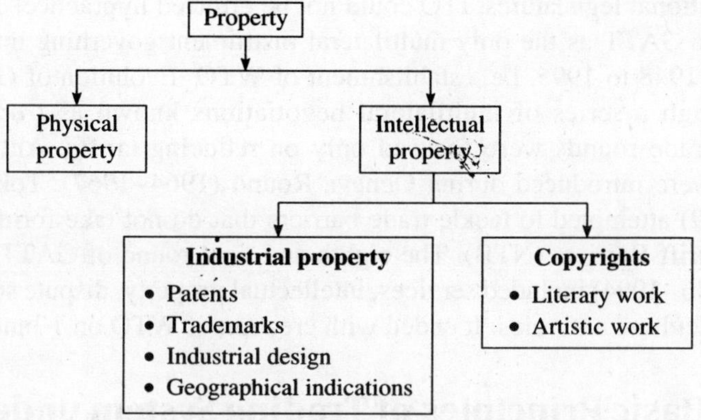

Figure 1.1 Classification of Property.

1.2 INTRODUCTION OF WTO

World Trade Organization (WTO) came into being on 1 January 1995. It is an international organization aimed at liberalizing trade. WTO also acts as a forum for governments to negotiate trade agreements and settle trade disputes by operating a system of trade rules. By the start of 2010, 153 governments were member of WTO and 28 governments were pursuing accession to WTO. WTO is basically a negotiating forum, where trade problems faced by member countries are sorted out by negotiations. The major chunk of WTO's current work came from the Uruguay Round (1986–1994 negotiations) and present negotiations are largely based on "Doha Development Agenda", initiated in 2001. Legal ground-rules for international trade are provided by WTO agreements which are at the core of WTO. These agreements are contracts, binding governments to keep their trade policies within the agreed limits.

1.2.1 History

After World War II, there was an attempt to create third institution to handle the trade side of international economic co-operation along with other two institutions, i.e. the World Bank and the International Monetary Fund. This institution was to be named as International Trade Organization (ITO) and was proposed as a specialized agency of the United Nations. But before that, 15 countries had begun talks in December 1947 to reduce and bind custom tariffs. Ultimately this group expanded to 23 and a tariff agreement came into effect on 30 June 1948 with the name of General Agreements on Tariffs and Trade (GATT). Founding members of GATT were also a part of ITO charter negotiations. These founding members were in favour of accepting, swiftly and provisionally, some of the trade rules of the draft. Although ITO character was finally agreed upon in Havana in March 1948, but because of non-ratification by some national legislatures, ITO could not be effected in practice. This paved the way for GATT as the only multilateral instrument governing international trade from 1948 to 1995, i.e. establishment of WTO. Evolution of GATT took place through a series of multilateral negotiations known as *trade rounds*. First five trade rounds were focused only on reducing tariffs. Anti-dumping measures were introduced during Geneva Round (1964–1967). Tokyo Round (1973–1979) attempted to tackle trade barriers that do not take form of tariffs, i.e. Non Tariff Barriers (NTB). The eighth and final round of GATT (Uruguay Round: 1986–1994) included services, intellectual property, dispute settlements, textile, agriculture and rules. It ended with creation of WTO on 1 January 1995.

1.2.2 Basic Principles of Trading System under WTO

Trading system of WTO is based on principles, such as trade without discrimination, freer trade, predictability, promoting fair competition and encouragement to development and economic reforms. Most important principle of trade without discrimination includes Most Favoured Nation (MFN) and National Treatment. Under MFN, each member treats all the other members equally as *most favoured* trading partners. If a country improves the benefits that it gives to one trading partner, it has to give the same treatment to all other WTO members as well. National treatment calls for treating imported and locally produced goods equally—at least after the foreign goods have entered the market.

1.2.3 Structure of WTO Agreements

Umbrella agreement of WTO includes agreements pertaining to:

- Goods
- Services
- Intellectual property

Basic principles concerning these three areas are as follows:

- General Agreement on Tariffs and Trade (GATT): Goods
- General Agreement on Trade in Services (GATS): Services
- Trade Related Intellectual Property Rights (TRIPS): Intellectual Property

GATT and GATS are supported by additional details pertaining to other goods agreements and annexes, and service annexes, respectively. Further, market access commitments related to schedules of commitments of various countries are also a part of WTO structure. For settling trade disputes, dispute settlement is included and transparency of various members is ensured through trade policy reviews.

As mentioned above, these agreements and annexes deal with a number of specific issues, for goods, i.e. under (GATT) the additional details include:

- Agriculture
- Health regulations of farm products (Sanitary and Phyto sanitary measures)
- Textiles and clothing
- Product standards (Technical barriers to trade)
- Investment measures (Trade-related investment measures)
- Anti-dumping measures
- Customs valuation methods
- Reshipment inspection
- Rules of origin
- Import licensing
- Subsidies and counter-measures
- Safeguards

In case of services, GATS annexes include:

- Movement of Natural Persons
- Air Transport
- Financial Services
- Shipping
- Telecommunications

1.2.4 Dispute Settlement

Dispute settlement has been termed as central pillar of the multilateral trading system. Rule-based system of WTO is made more effective by the means of settling disputes, ensuring more secure and predictable trading system. The system is based on clearly defined rules, with time tables for completing a case. First rulings are made by a panel, and endorsed/rejected by WTO's full membership. Disputes, however, are settled through consultations. By July 2005, only about 130 of the nearly 3320 cases had reached the full panel process. The remaining cases was either settled *out of the court* or being still solved under consultation process.

1.2.5 Trade Policy Reviews

For ensuring transparency, trade policy review mechanism is in place in WTO. Transparency is ensured in two ways, firstly, governments have to inform the

WTO and the fellow members of specific measures, policies or laws through regular notifications, and the WTO conducts regular reviews of individual countries trade policies. Frequency of the reviews depends on the size of the country (in terms of their share of world trade):

- European Union, USA, Japan and Canada are examined approximately once every two years.
- Next 16 countries are examined every four years
- The remaining countries are reviewed every six years

1.3 AGREEMENT ON TRIPS

In its preamble itself, agreement on TRIPS identifies Intellectual Property Rights as private rights. Agreement on TRIPS is aimed at doing way with the impediments to international trade, and takes into account the need for promoting effectiveness and adequacy of protection of intellectual property rights, but at the same time supports the logic that the steps taken in the direction of enforcing intellectual property rights do not emerge as the barriers to trade. With the above-mentioned aims, agreement on TRIPS emphasized for the need for new rules that included:

1. The applicability of the basic principles of GATT along with the relevant international intellectual property agreements and conventions
2. Providing adequate standards and principles encompassing the availability, scope and use of trade-related intellectual property rights
3. Providing effective and appropriate means for enforcing of trade-related intellectual property rights by factoring in the differences in legal systems across the nations
4. Providing effective and prompt procedures for preventing the disputes between governments, and putting in place the mechanism of dispute settlements.

Agreement on TRIPS has been divided into seven parts as shown in Table 1.1 and the important issues concerning the present text are being discussed in the following sections.

1.3.1 Part I—General Provisions and Basic Principles of TRIPS

General provisions and basic principles of TRIPS have been covered in Part I of the agreement. These provisions and principles form the basis of understanding and interpreting the further provisions made under TRIPS. Articles 1 to 8 provide the details of these provisions and the principles. Salient provisions and principles are being discussed as follows:

Table 1.1 Scheme of Agreement on TRIPS under WTO

Part I	General Provisions and Basic Principles
Part II	**Standards Concerning the Availability, Scope and Use of Intellectual Property Rights**
1.	Copyright and Related Rights
2.	Trade Marks
3.	Geographical Indications
4.	Industrial Designs
5.	Patents
6	Layout-Designs (Topographies) of Integrated Circuits
7.	Protection of Undisclosed Information
8.	Control of Anti-Competitive Practices in Contractual Licenses
Part III	**Enforcement of Intellectual Property Rights**
1.	General Obligations
2.	Civil and Administrative Procedures and Remedies
3.	Provisional Measures
4.	Special Requirements Related to Border Measures
5.	Criminal Procedures
Part IV	**Acquisition and Maintenance of Intellectual Property Rights and Related *Inter-Partes* Procedures**
Part V	**Dispute Prevention and Settlement**
Part VI	**Transitional Arrangements**
Part VII	**Institutional Arrangements; Final Provisions**

Article 1 of the agreement of TRIPS deals with 'Nature and Scope of Obligations'. This Article provides that members may go for more extensive protection than required by the agreement provided that such protection does not contravene the provisions of the agreement. Article 1 provides freedom to the member countries to determine the appropriate method of implementing the provisions of this Agreement within their own legal system and practice. Further, Article 1 identifies all categories of intellectual property that are the subject of Sections 1 through 7 of Part II. These categories of intellectual property have been listed as follows:

- Copyrights
- Trade Marks
- Geographical Indications
- Industrial Designs
- Patents
- Layout-Designs (Topographies) of Integrated Circuits
- Protection of Undisclosed Information

Article 2 of agreement on TRIPS deals with 'Intellectual Property Conventions'. This provision of the agreement ensures the continuity of the following conventions:

- Paris Convention dealing with protection of Industrial Property
- Berne Convention related to protection of Literary and Artistic works
- Rome Convention dealing with the protection of Performers, Producers of Phonograms and Broadcasting Organizations
- Treaty on Intellectual Property in respect of Integrated Circuits adopted at Washington

Article 3 of Agreement on TRIPS deals with the issue of 'National Treatment'. According to this article, each Member shall accord to the nationals of other Members treatment no less favourable than that it accords to its own nationals regarding the protection of intellectual property. Some exceptions provided in this regard include the exceptions already provided in, the Paris Convention (1967), the Berne Convention (1971), the Rome Convention or the Treaty on Intellectual Property in Respect of Integrated Circuits. In case of performers, producers of phonograms and broadcasting organizations, this obligation is only applicable in respect of the rights provided under this Agreement.

Article 4 deals with 'Most Favoured Nation Treatment'. This article provides that with regard to the protection of intellectual property, any advantage, favour, privilege or immunity granted by a member to the nationals of any other country shall be accorded immediately and unconditionally to the nationals of all other members. Members are exempted from this obligation if they have accorded any advantage, favour, privilege or immunity that are:

- Deriving from international agreements on judicial assistance or law enforcement of a general nature and not particularly confined to the protection of intellectual property
- Granted in accordance with the provisions of the Berne Convention (1971) or the Rome Convention authorizing that the treatment accorded be a function not of national treatment, but of the treatment accorded in another country
- In respect of the rights of performers, producers of phonograms and broadcasting organizations not provided under this Agreement
- Deriving from international agreements related to the protection of intellectual property which entered into force before the implementation of the WTO Agreement, subject to the condition that such agreements are notified to the Council for TRIPS, and do not lead to an arbitrary or unjustifiable discrimination against nationals of other member countries.

Article 7 of the agreement on TRIPS provides that the purpose of protection and enforcement of intellectual property rights is to promote the technological innovation, transfer of technology and technology dissemination in a manner that is advantageous for the creators as well as the users of technological knowledge while ensuring social and economic welfare along with the balance of rights and obligations among the trading members.

Article 8 provides that members may, in formulating or amending their laws and regulations, adopt measures necessary for protecting public health and nutrition, and for promoting the public interest in sectors of vital importance to their development in socio-economic and technological domains, provided that such measures are consistent with the provisions of the agreement. Further, this article identifies the appropriate measures that may be needed to prevent the abuse of intellectual property rights by right holders or the resort to practices which unreasonably restrain trade or adversely affect the international transfer of technology.

1.3.2 Part II—Standards Concerning the Availability, Scope and Use of Intellectual Property Rights

Standards concerning the availability, scope and use of IPRs have been given in Part II of the agreement on TRIPS. First seven sections of Part II deal with seven types of IPRs discussed in the previous section, and Section 8 deals with control of anti-competitive practices in contractual licenses. Various sections of Part II are being introduced as follows:

Copyright and Related Rights

Article 9 of agreement on TRIPS provides that members shall abide by Articles 1 to 21 of the Berne Convention (1971) as well as the Appendix thereto. However, members shall not have rights or obligations under this Agreement in respect of the rights conferred under Article 6b is of that Convention or of the rights derived therefrom. Detailed discussion on copyright and related rights has been presented in Chapter 4 of this book.

Trade Marks

Article 15 of agreement on TRIPS provides the definition of protectable subject matter as any sign, or any combination of signs, capable of distinguishing the goods or services of one undertaking from those of other undertakings, shall be capable of constituting a trade mark. Such signs, in particular words including personal names, letters, numerals, figurative elements and combinations of colours as well as any combination of such signs, shall be eligible for registration as trade marks. Where signs are not inherently capable of distinguishing the relevant goods or services, members may make registrability depend on distinctiveness acquired through use. Members may require, as a condition of registration, that signs be visually perceptible. Detailed discussion on trade marks has been presented in Chapter 5 of this book.

Geographical Indications

Article 22 of agreement on TRIPS provides the definition of geographical indication as indications which identify a good as originating in the territory of a member, or a region or locality in that territory, where a given quality, reputation or other characteristic of the good is essentially attributable to its geographical origin. Detailed discussion on geographical indications has been presented in Chapter 7 of this book.

Industrial Designs

Article 25 of agreement on TRIPS requires the members to provide for the protection of independently created industrial designs that are new or original. Members may provide that designs are not new or original, if they do not significantly differ from known designs or combinations of known design features. Members may provide that such protection shall not extend to designs dictated essentially by technical or functional considerations. Chapter 6 of this book presents a discussion on industrial designs.

Patents

Article 27 of agreement on TRIPS provides that patents shall be available for any inventions, whether products or processes, in all fields of technology, provided that they are new, involve an inventive step, and are capable of industrial application. Detailed discussion on the patents has been presented in Chapter 2 and Chapter 3 of this book.

Layout-Designs (Topographies) of Integrated Circuits

Article 35 of agreement on TRIPS provides protection to the layout-designs (topographies) of integrated circuits in accordance with Articles 2 through 7 (other than paragraph 3 of Article 6), Article 12 and paragraph 3 of Article 16 of the Treaty on Intellectual Property in Respect of Integrated Circuits. For more details one can refer Chapter 6 of this book.

Protection of Undisclosed Information

Article 39 of agreement on TRIPS deals with protection of undisclosed information, sometimes also referred to as trade secrets. According to this article natural and legal persons shall have the possibility of preventing information lawfully within their control from being disclosed to, acquired by, or used by others without their consent in a manner contrary to honest commercial practices so long as such information:

- Is secret in the sense that it is not, as a body or in the precise configuration and assembly of its components, generally known among or readily accessible to persons within the circles that normally deal with the kind of information in question

- Has commercial value, because it is a secret
- Is subject to reasonable steps under the circumstances, by the person lawfully in control of the information, to keep it secret.

1.3.3 Part III—Enforcement of Intellectual Property Rights

Part III of agreement on TRIPS deals with enforcement of IPRs. Article 41 of agreement on TRIPS provides that members shall ensure the enforcement of procedures specified in Part III are part of the national law so as to facilitate effective action against any act of infringement of intellectual property rights in a manner that ensures speedy remedies to thwart infringements and remedies which form a deterrent to further infringements. At the same time, it should be ensured that the application of such procedures should not lead to the creation of barriers to legitimate trade and adequate safeguards are in place for preventing their abuse. Procedures concerning the enforcement of intellectual property rights should be fair and equitable. Implementation of the procedures should not be complicated, costly and unreasonably long process.

1.3.4 Part IV—Acquisition and Maintenance of Intellectual Property Rights and Related *Inter-Partes* Procedures

Article 62 mentioned in the Part IV of agreement on TRIPS requires compliance with reasonable procedures and formalities for the acquisition and maintenance of copyright and related rights, trade marks, industrial designs, patents and integrated circuits layout designs. Further, it is required that such procedures and formalities shall be consistent with the provisions of the agreement on TRIPS. Moreover, this article provides that *inter partes* procedures, such as opposition, revocation and cancellation, shall be governed by the general principles set out in agreement on TRIPS.

1.3.5 Part V—Dispute Prevention and Settlement

Issue of dispute prevention and settlement has been discussed in Part V of agreement on TRIPS. Article 63 of agreement on TRIPS deals with transparency, and provides that laws and regulations, final judicial decisions and administrative rulings, made effective by a member pertaining to the subject matter of TRIPS shall be published and made available to the general public in the national language so that the governments and various right holders are well versed with the provisions of the TRIPS. This part is aimed at lowering the likelihood of disputes among the members by means of spreading awareness among the general masses.

Article 64 of TRIPS agreement deals with the dispute settlement mandates that the provisions of Articles XXII and XXIII of GATT 1994 as explained and applied by the Dispute Settlement Understanding shall be applicable to consultations and the dispute settlement under TRIPS Agreement, except in case of specific provisions.

1.3.6 Part VI—Transitional Arrangements and Part VII—Institutional Arrangements; Final Provisions

Part VI provides for the transitional arrangements regarding the time frame for compliance to the provisions of agreement on TRIPS and **Part VII** asserts the supremacy of the Council on TRIPS as article 68 states that the Council for TRIPS shall monitor the operation of this Agreement and, in particular, members' compliance with their obligations hereunder, and shall afford members the opportunity of consulting on matters relating to the trade-related aspects of intellectual property rights.

1.4 MINISTERIAL CONFERENCES

1.4.1 First Ministerial Conference—Singapore

First biennial Ministerial Conference, as provided in Article IV of WTO, was held in Singapore from 9 December to 13 December 1996. The conference emphasized its commitment to core labour standards and rejected the use of labour standards for protectionist purposes. It was recognized that Regional Trade Agreements (RTAs) were on the rise. Primacy of multilateral trading system was reaffirmed and emphasis was laid on the fact that RTAs should be consistent with the provisions of WTO. Apart from this, issues related to Textile and Clothing, Trade and Environment and Service Negotiations were also discussed. It is important to mention that three working groups were set in Singapore Ministerial Conference to discuss the following issues:

- Trade and Investment
- Competition Policy
- Transparency in Government Procurement

Moreover, WTO Goods Council was directed to simplify the trade procedure and the issue was termed as "Trade Facilitation". These four issues are referred to as "Singapore Issues". A declaration on Trade in Information Technology Products was also undertaken in the conference. Member countries were asked to evolve trade regimes so that market access for information technology products. Further, the member countries were required to eliminate custom duties and other duties/charges with respect to certain items as per the provisions of Article II: 1(b) of GATT.

1.4.2 Second Ministerial Conference—Geneva

Second Ministerial Conference of WTO was held in Geneva (Switzerland) from 30 November–2 December 1998. The conference underlined the importance of multilateral rule-based trading system. Concluded negotiations on basic telecommunication and financial services were welcomed at the conference. Growth of Electronic commerce was recognized at the conference and it was decided to establish a comprehensive work programme to examine the trade related issues concerning global Electronic Commerce.

1.4.3 Third Ministerial Conference—Seattle

Third Ministerial Conference was held in Seattle (United States of America) from 30 November to 3 December 1999. Major issues on the agenda for this conference were agriculture, textiles, anti-dumping, and core labour standards. Huge protest and demonstrations were witnessed during the conference and talks were abandoned without any ministerial declaration.

1.4.4 Fourth Ministerial Conference—Doha

In the wake of failure at Seattle, fourth Ministerial Conference of WTO was held in Doha (Qatar) from 9 November–13 November 2001. Major issues on the agenda during the conference were TRIPS and Public Health, along with the concerns of the developing and Least Developed Countries regarding the implementation of WTO. Doha Development Round was started with lot of expectations in the conference.

Major issues of Doha Round are being listed as follows:

- Agriculture
- Non-Agricultural Market Access (NAMA)
- Intellectual Property
- Trade and Environment
- Trade Facilitation
- E-Commerce
- Dispute Settlement

Known as Doha Development Agenda, the latest round of trade negotiations at WTO is aimed to achieve reforms in the international trading system with fundamental objective to enhance the trading opportunities for the developing nations. Development was the main plank of Doha Round of talks.

WTO Doha Development Trade Round collapsed in 2006, on account of the deadlock between the developing nations and the developed nations.

Developed nations were interested in the access to domestic markets of the developing countries. Developing nations insisted on the corrections in the structural flaws and distortions in the trading system, largely on account of the subsidized products of the developed nations.

Doha talks have been held in series of rounds since their initiation. The process has suffered a number of setbacks, and nothing conclusive has come out of the negotiations till date.

Declaration of the TRIPS Agreement and Public Health at Doha

Trade ministers of the member countries recognized the problems in the domain of public health faced by the developing and Least Developed Countries (LDCs). It was declared that TRIPS will be part of the initiatives and actions taken at National and International level for finding out solutions to the issue. While the importance of Intellectual Property (IP) protection was recognized for the development of new medicines, at the same time concerns were registered regarding the high price of the medicines on account of IP protection, especially in the countries that lack pharmaceutical manufacturing facilities. An agreement prevailed in the member countries that TRIPS should not prevent the countries from acting in the domain of health for public interest. On this account, flexibilities were provided in the WTO arrangement. Major issues of flexibility provided in the decision are being listed as follows:

- Each member was given right to grant compulsory licenses and the grounds used for granting such licenses were left to the discretion of the concerned member.
- Right to determine a national emergency or other circumstance of extreme emergency was given to the members. Specifically, HIV/AIDS, tuberculosis, malaria and other epidemics were mentioned for the purpose.
- Members were given freedom to establish their own regimes regarding the exhaustion of IPRs.

1.4.5 Fifth Ministerial Conference—Cancun

Fifth Ministerial Conference was held in Cancun (Mexico) from 10 September to 14 September 2003. The main agenda of the conference was to take stock of the progress in negotiations as well as the progress made under Doha Development Agenda. Not much could be achieved in the conference and ministerial statement adopted at the end of the conference called for setting a deadline for the conclusions of the negotiations and Doha Declaration and Decisions were reaffirmed.

1.4.6 Sixth Ministerial Conference—Hong Kong

Sixth Ministerial Conference of WTO was held in Hong Kong, China from 13 December to 18 December 2005. This conference was stated to be crucial for the conclusion of negotiations on Doha Development Agenda. Ministerial Declaration of the conference resolved to complete Doha Work Programme and to conclude related negotiations by 2006. Major decisions taken in the conference were reduction in domestic support in agriculture and elimination of all forms of export subsidies by the end of 2013.

1.4.7 Seventh Ministerial Conference—Geneva

Seventh Ministerial Conference was held in Geneva from 30 November to 2 December 2009. As the conference was preceded by the global economic slowdown, the theme of the conference was "The WTO, the Multilateral Trading System and the Current Global Economic Environment". This conference was not taken up as negotiation platform but as an opportunity to review the working of WTO including the progress on the Doha Round Talks.

1.4.8 Eighth Ministerial Conference—Geneva

Geneva was the host city for the Eighth Ministerial Conference held from 15 December to 17 December 2011. Apart from the plenary session, working sessions were held on the following themes:

- Importance of the Multilateral Trading System and the WTO
- Trade and Development
- Doha Development Agenda

Major conference issues included Intellectual Property, Electronic Commerce, Food Security, Government Procurement, and Trade Monitoring. Conference also saw the trade ministers of the member countries adopt a waiver that enabled the developed and the developing countries to provide preferential treatment to services and service supplier of Least Developed Country members. It was decided that this waiver will continue till 2026.

1.5 SUMMARY

Intellectual property rights are the creations of human mind. Property can be broadly classified into two categories, i.e. physical property and intellectual property. Intellectual property can be divided further into two categories—industrial property and copyrights. Industrial property includes patents, trade marks, industrial designs, geographical indications, layout of integrated circuits and undisclosed information. World Trade Organization (WTO) came into being on 1 January 1995. WTO acts as a forum for governments to negotiate trade agreements and settle trade disputes by operating a system of trade rules. Major agreements under WTO include GATT, GATS and TRIPS. Agreement on TRIPS sets standards for the grant and protection of intellectual property. TRIPS has been divided into seven parts and deals with the aspects of intellectual property in detail.

CASE STUDY—CHINA ENTERS WTO

On 11 December 2001, China was formally inducted into WTO. It took around 15 years of negotiations with China for facilitating entry, and a bulky 900 pages of legal text was prepared that was sent to 142 member (in 2001) countries of WTO for formal acceptance. As the consequence of the negotiations, China agreed to undertake a number of commitments for opening up and liberalizing its economy. This effort is basically aimed at better integration with the world economy and presenting a more predictable environment for trade and foreign investments in compliance to WTO rules. It was not the case that China was not doing well even without membership of WTO. According to the international trade statistics in 2000, China was the seventh largest exporter (with 3.9 percent share of global exports) and eighth largest importer (3.4 percent share of global imports) of merchandise trade. For commercial services, China stood 12th in terms of exports (with 2.1 percent share of global exports) and tenth in terms of imports (2.5 percent share in global imports). For entering into WTO, China made a number of commitments:

- Providing non-discriminatory treatment to all WTO members
- Elimination of dual pricing and differential treatment offered to good produced for sale in China and those produced for exports
- Not using price controls for the purpose of affording protection to domestic players
- Implementing WTO agreement in an effective and uniform manner through the revisions of existing laws and enactment of new legislations
- Implementing TRIPS from the date of accession

China could have avoided this long wait of joining WTO, it is worth noticing that China was on of the 23 original signatories of the General Agreement on Tariff and Trade (GATT) in 1948. It was only after revolution of 1949 that government in Taiwan made the announcement of China leaving GATT system. It was the year of 1986 that China expressed its wish to resume its status as a GATT contracting party. Joining back was not an easy task and decision; the possible factors that kept China away from GATT for so long are being listed as follows:

- Challenge before the inefficient farm sector of China with the fear of loss of source of livelihood for 10 million farmers
- Banking sector in China which was afraid of being eaten away by the competition from the foreign banks
- Security agencies including People's Liberation Army that was uncomfortable with the free flow of western ideas and ways of working as this could have made their job of maintaining the longevity of one party communist state more difficult
- Lack of awareness about WTO in China

Accession of China is being seen as a win-win situation for China and WTO as described by the then Director General of WTO "with China's membership, the WTO will take a major step towards becoming a truly world organization. The near-universal acceptance of its rule-based system will serve a pivotal role in underpinning global economic cooperation".

ISSUES FOR DISCUSSION

1. Do you think WTO is merely a trade governing body or its effects spread far beyond trade?
2. What type of impact will be there on other member countries with the accession of China to WTO?
3. What factors could have led China to join back WTO?

Discussion Questions

1. Discuss in detail the genesis and creation of WTO.
2. Differentiate between "Intellectual Property" and "Physical Property".
3. Discuss in detail the aims of agreement on TRIPS.
4. Elaborate the general provisions and principles of TRIPS?
5. What do you understand by 'Most Favoured Nation Treatment'?
6. What can be classified as undisclosed information? Is any protection available under TRIPS for protecting undisclosed information?
7. Write short note on the following:
   (a) Dispute Settlement and Prevention under TRIPS
   (b) Classification of Intellectual Property
   (c) Structure of WTO agreements
   (d) "Protection of Intellectual Property gives a push to new inventions". Comment on the statement.

Objective Type Questions

Tick the right answer in given multiple-choice questions:

1. Which of the following treaty deals with protection of industrial property
   (a) Rome (b) Berne (c) Paris (d) Washington
2. Which of the following treaty deals with protection of literary and artistic works
   (a) Rome (b) Berne (c) Paris (d) Washington
3. Which of the following treaty deals with protection of performers, producers of phonograms and broadcasting organizations
   (a) Rome (b) Berne (c) Paris (d) Washington

4. WTO came into being in
   (a) 1998 (b) 1995 (c) 1986 (d) 1980
5. Eighth and final round of GATT was held at
   (a) Havana (b) Tokyo (c) Uruguay (d) Sweden
6. Which of the following is not termed as industrial property
   (a) Patents (b) Trade marks (c) Copyrights (d) Industrial designs
7. Trade review of Japan is done every
   (a) One year (b) Two years (c) Three years (d) Four years
8. Which of the following agreement covers services under WTO?
   (a) TRIPS (b) GATT (c) GATS (d) None of these
9. Which of the following agreement covers goods under WTO?
   (a) TRIPS (b) GATT (c) GATS (d) None of these
10. Which of the following agreement covers intellectual property under WTO?
    (a) TRIPS (b) GATT (c) GATS (d) None of these

Mark TRUE or FALSE against given statements:

1. Uruguay round was the longest and final round of GATT. (True/False)
2. TRIPS deals with services. (True/False)
3. Patent can be termed as an industrial property. (True/False)
4. Copyright is not an industrial property. (True/False)
5. China is not a member of WTO. (True/False)

Websites

1. www.wto.org
2. www.wipo.int

CHAPTER 2

Fundamentals of Patent

We all today are in the knowledge era. The intellectual property created by an organization or an individual would decide its standing in the long run. Those producing intellectual property in the form of inventions need to be motivated and rewarded for their effort. The patents provide one such reward for the invention done, and the respective national patent offices maintain a record of the complete detail of technology of invented product. This motivates the individuals or organizations to do innovations and invent newer things rather than 'reinventing the wheel'. This helps in making the world a better place to live in as the individuals, groups and organizations exert more to innovate and invent. In return, they expect incentive and recognition of their hard work by way of grant of the patent.

2.1 WHAT IS A PATENT?

In case of invention of product, which has a manufacturing component in it, the inventor/s has two choices, viz. apply for patent or maintain it as a trade secret. The patent will provide an exclusive legal right for a limited period to the inventor (called patentee). In case of trade secret, the inventor may have rights over his innovation for infinite period provided s/he maintains the secrecy of the invention.

A patent is "an intellectual property right relating to inventions and is the grant of exclusive right, for limited period, provided by the Government to the patentee, in exchange of full disclosure of his invention, for excluding others, from making, using, selling, importing the patented product or process producing that product for those purposes".[1] WIPO (World Intellectual Property Organization) defines patent as an exclusive right granted in respect of an invention, which may be a product or a process, that provides a new and inventive way of doing something, or offers a new and inventive technical solution to a problem. The examples of patent are telephone, radio, optical fibre, ipod and ballpoint pens.

1. http://www.ipindia.nic.in

The patent is a territorial right, i.e. the patent is granted by respective countries for enforcement in their nation. There is no such thing like world patent. The patent is granted for 20 years.

2.2 HISTORY OF PATENT IN INDIA

The Act VI of 1856	– Protection of Invention based on the British Patent Law of 1852
The Patents and Designs Protection Act, 1872	
The Inventions and Designs Act, 1883	
Indian Patents and Designs Act, 1911	– British rulers enacted separate rules for India to protect the interests of the inventors
The Patents Bill, 1953 and The Patents Bill, 1965	– Lapsed due to political reasons
Indian Patents Act, 1970	– Comprehensive law on patent
The Repealing and Amending Act, 1974	– Amendments to Patent Act
The Delegated Legislation Provisions (Amendment) Act, 1985	
The Patents (Amendment) Act, 1999	
The Patents (Amendment) Act, 2002	
The Patents (Amendment) Act, 2005	

2.3 CONDITIONS FOR GRANT OF PATENT

An innovation for being patentable has to satisfy three conditions viz.

1. **Novelty:** The invention must be first of its kinds. The details of the invention should not have been published anywhere in the world before the date of filing of the patent application. For example, in case of turmeric patent granted by United States Patent Office, it was revoked on the proof provided by CSIR (Council of Scientific and Industrial Research) that the medicative value of turmeric was already published in ancient Indian Vedic scripture.
2. **Non-obvious:** The invention to be filed in patent application should not be obvious to a person skilled in the art on the basis of prior knowledge, publications or patents, i.e. there should not be cosmetic changes to highlight the newness of the product or process. For example, merely changing the positioning of components of the product or colour of the product will be an obvious change and

though it will appear new, but actually an expert in the field shall make out its non-patentability.

3. **Useful:** The invention must be capable of industrial application and not harmful to the society. Any destructive technology having potential of adverse effect on masses may not be considered patentable.

2.4 INVENTIONS THOSE ARE NOT PATENTABLE

According to Section 3 and Section 4 of Indian Patent Act, 1970, and subsequent amendments, following "are not patentable as they are not inventions within the meaning of this Act:

1. An invention which is frivolous or that claims anything which is contrary to well-established natural laws.
2. An invention the primary or intended use or commercial exploitation of which could be contrary public order or morality or which causes serious prejudice to human, animal or plant life or health or to the environment.
3. The mere discovery of a scientific principle or the formulation of an abstract theory or discovery of any living being or non-living substances occurring in nature.
4. The mere discovery of a new form of a known substance which does not result in the enhancement of the known efficacy of that substance or the mere discovery of a new property or new use for a known substance or of the mere use of a known process, machine or apparatus unless such known process results in a new product or employs at least one new reactant.
5. A substance obtained by a mere admixture resulting only in the aggregation of the properties of the components thereof or a process for producing such substance.
6. The mere arrangement or re-arrangement or duplication of known devices each functioning independently of one another in a known way.
7. A method of agriculture or horticulture.
8. Any process for the medicinal, surgical, curative, prophylactic or other treatment of human beings or any process for a similar treatment of animals to render them free of disease or to increase their economic value or that of their products.
9. Plants and animals in whole or any part thereof other than micro-organisms, but including seeds, varieties and species and essentially biological processes production or propagation of plants and animals.
10. A mathematical or business method or a computer programme per se or algorithms.

11. A literary, dramatic, musical or artistic work or any other aesthetic creation whatsoever including cinematographic works and television productions.
12. A mere scheme or rule or method of performing mental act or method of playing game.
13. A presentation of information.
14. Topography of integrated circuits.
15. An invention which in effect, is traditional knowledge or which is an aggregation or duplication of known properties of traditionally known component or components.
16. Inventions relating to atomic energy and inventions prejudicial to the interest of security of India".[2]

2.5 PROCESS AND PRODUCT PATENT

Each invention involves some process to make a product. The way the product is made by adding constituents under certain conditions, viz. temperature and pressure is a subject matter of process patent. In such cases one product may have 'n' ways of making it and all these ways may be patentable through process patent, in case that nation allows for process patent in that category of product. Therefore, one product may have many process patents. For Example, X, Y and Z are constituents to make a product 'D' at temperature 'T' and pressure 'P' so one process would be:

$$X + Y + Z \xrightarrow{T,P} D$$

The other ways for making product 'D' may be:

$$X_1 + Y + Z \xrightarrow{T,P} D$$
$$X + Y_1 + Z \xrightarrow{T,P} D$$
$$X + Y + Z_1 \xrightarrow{T,P} D$$
$$X_1 + Y_1 + Z_1 \xrightarrow{T,P} D$$
$$X + Y + Z \xrightarrow{T_1,P_1} D$$

X_1, Y_1 and Z_1 are newer or substitute constituents for X, Y and Z, respectively. Similarly T_1 and P_1 are different temperature and pressure from the previous one. The same product 'D' is being manufactured from different processes.

However, more and more nations are shifting to a product patent regime from process patent regime. In product patent it is not only the process of producing/manufacturing that has to be different, but also it should result in a new product.

2. http://ipindia.nic.in/ipr/patent/patents_filing.pdf

$$X_1 + Y + Z \xrightarrow{T_1, P_1} D_1$$
$$X + Y_1 + Z \xrightarrow{T_2, P_2} D_2$$
$$X + Y + Z_1 \xrightarrow{T_3, P_3} D_3$$

So process patent is same product, different process, whereas product patent is different product, different process. As a corollary, if somebody has acquired product patent it is implied that s/he has all privileges and rights of a process patent.

2.6 SPECIFICATION

The technical description of the invention is called specification. Its content includes technical details, drawing and other specific details about the invention. It is important document in patent application. There are two types of specification, viz. provisional specification and complete specification.

Provisional specification is filed by the inventor when he is about to complete his invention. In India, since the Patent Law is based on 'first-to-file' principle, it is advisable to file provisional specification with the Patent Office as the inventor has done sufficient work and is soon to file patent application for its award. The provisional specification is akin to 'making a railway reservation in advance' to book one's seat in advance. Once a provisional specification is filed, that particular invention is booked at your name for a certain period and inventor may complete his invention with full peace of mind.

Complete Specification is the full description of the invention along with all claims related to invention. It includes title; complete detail of process of invention including full detail of technology involved in it, if any; the complete detail of the best method of performing the invention which is known to the applicant and for which s/he is entitled to claim protection; all claims regarding scope of that particular invention and drawing, if any. The complete specification has to be filled within twelve months of the date of filing provisional specification. This period is extendable by another three months on the discretion of the Controller. There is an upper limit for filing complete specification as one specific area of research cannot be blocked for other inventors sine die which may prove demotivating for other innovators who are working in same/similar fields. Therefore, if inventor does not file complete specification after expiry of 15 months, the patent application of that inventor is deemed to have been abandoned.

The provisional specification should be filed to the patent office with caution that the inventor is confident that s/he shall be able to file complete specification before next twelve months. In case the inventor fails to do so, then the topic and field of research is publicly known and may be used by some individual or agency for his personal gains, such as publishing paper or filing patent in its name. The credibility of the inventor with the patent authorities is lost, besides losing money and time spent on filing the provisional specification.

2.7 PROCEDURE FOR GRANT OF PATENT

A series of steps are involved in filing of the patent (Figure 2.1). Section 6 to Section 11 of Chapter III of the Patents Act, 1970 lists conditions to be satisfied by the applicant for submission of application. Chapter IV lists the conditions for publication and examination of applications. Chapter V and VIII of the Patents Act, 1970 provides for Opposition to grant of patents, and Grant and sealing of patents, respectively.

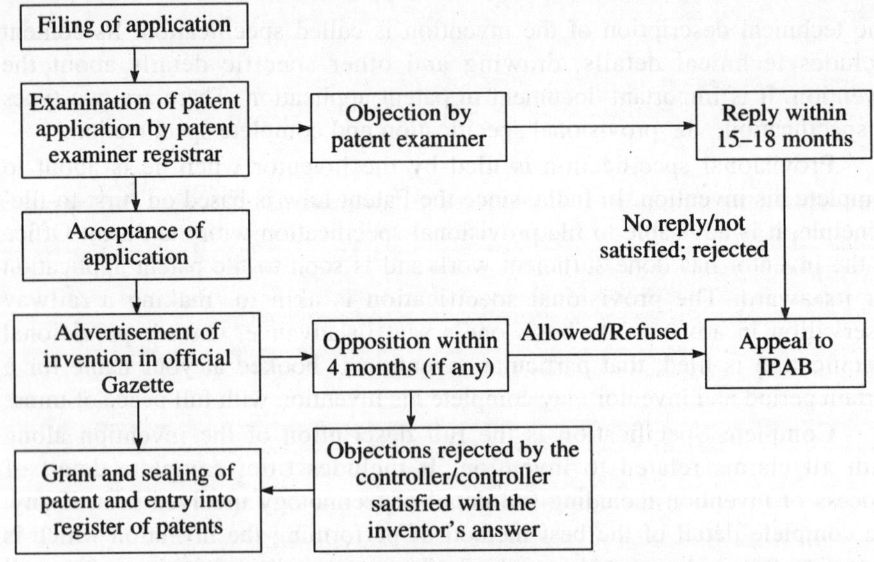

Figure 2.1 Procedure for Grant of Patent.

The ***first step*** in procedure for the grant of patent is locating appropriate patent office (Table 2.1) for filing the patent application that is appropriate to your place of work. Then application is to be submitted by filling prescribed patent form along with prescribed fee. The provisional or complete specification should also be attached along with patent form as it is essential part of the application.

According to Section 6 of Indian Patent Act, 1970 and subsequent amendments, "following persons may file patent application:

(a) By any person claiming to be the true and first inventor of the invention;

(b) By any person being the assignee of the person claiming to be the true and first inventor in respect of the right to make such an application;

Table 2.1 Territorial Jurisdiction of Patent Offices

Patent Office	*Territorial Jurisdiction*
Patent Office, Mumbai	The States of Maharashtra, Gujarat, Madhya Pradesh and Goa, Daman & Diu and Dadra & Nagar Haveli.
Patent Office, Chennai	The Sates of Andhra Pradesh, Kerala, Tamil Nadu, Pondicherry, Lakshadweep, Andaman & Nicobar Islands.
Patent Office, New Delhi	States of Haryana, Himachal Pradesh, Jammu & Kashmir, Punjab, Rajasthan and Uttar Pradesh, Chandigarh and Delhi.
Patent Office, Kolkata	The rest of India.

(c) By legal representative of any deceased person who immediately before his death was entitled to make such an application".[3]

A patent application may be made by any person alone or jointly with two or more number of persons. The following documents are required in filing patent application:

(i) Application form in duplicate (Form 1)
(ii) Provisional or complete specification in duplicate
(iii) Drawing in duplicate (if any)
(iv) Abstract of the invention in duplicate
(v) Information and undertaking listing the number, filling date and current status of each foreign patent application in duplicate (Form 3)
(vi) Declaration of inventorship where provisional specification is followed by complete specification or in case of PCT (Patent Cooperation Treaty) national phase application (Form 5)
(vii) Power of attorney (if filed through Patent Agent)
(viii) Fee (as per schedule I)

The ***second step*** is examination of application by patent examiners. The patent examiner does three basic checks in the application. Firstly, they check whether the application complies with the requirements of the Patent Act and Rules and the application is filled in proper way with all requisite information. Secondly, they check the legal ground of objection to the filed patent. Thirdly, they check whether the invention has already been published or claimed by any other person. In this check, it is interesting to note that though patent is granted nationally, i.e. it is valid only within the national boundaries of a country; the publication check is done globally. If it is found that the application claims are already published in any of the national or international journal, the applicant may not be granted the patent. This kind of search is also known as 'strategic

3. http://www.ipindia.nic.in

search' where the claim is cross-checked with huge existing patent databases and publication databases. A negative strategic search is positive sign for the inventor which means no matching databases were found and innovation is novel.

The ***third step*** is the communication to the inventor regarding objections, if any. During the strategic search, if some similarities/objections are found, it is communicated to the inventor for further clarification. Other cases include questions regarding drafting of specifications and claims, anticipation of any of the claims in prior publication, etc. The inventor has to give satisfactory reply or suggest amendments to the satisfaction of the Controller within fifteen months of the raising of objection by the patent office. This period may be extended to maximum three more months at the discretion of the Controller against plea of the inventor. If nothing is heard from the inventor at the expiry of fifteen months, the patent application is deemed to be abandoned. Also, if the Controller is not satisfied with the explanation/hearing of the applicant, the application is rejected. In case no objection is found at three basic search stage or inventor satisfactory answers to all the objections, the Controller accepts the patent application along with complete specification for next stage.

The ***fourth step*** is advertisement of the invention in official Gazette. The rationale behind the advertisement in official Gazette is that everyone knows about the particular patent and its claim; and if anyone has any kind of objection regarding it, they may file an opposition to it in the Patent Office. This is known as pre-grant opposition. Many countries including United States have only post-grant opposition. The opposition of the grant of patent must be filled within four months of the advertisement to which the inventor has to reply within one month. Therefore, the inventor has to be alert for next four months after the advertisement in official Gazette as he has to file a reply statement within one month from the date of receipt of copy of the objection.

As per Section 25 of the Patent Act, following are the "grounds for opposition for grant of patent:

1. The applicant for the patent wrongfully obtained the invention or any part thereof from him.
2. The invention claimed has been published before the filing date of patent application.
3. The invention has already been claimed as a part of complete specification of another application which was filed before the applicant's application.
4. The invention is publicly known or publicly used in India before the applicant's claim.
5. The invention, as claimed by the applicant, is obvious and does not involve any inventive step.
6. The subject of any claim of the complete specification is not an invention within the meaning of this Act, or is not patentable under the Act.

7. The complete specification does not sufficiently and clearly describes the invention or the method by which it is to be performed.
8. The applicant has not disclosed or given false information in the complete specification.
9. In case of convention application, the application was not made within twelve months from the date of the first application for protection of the invention made in a convention country by the applicant or a person from whom he derives title.
10. The complete specification does not disclose or wrongly mentions the source or geographical origin of biological material used for the invention.
11. The invention so far as claimed in any claim of the complete specification is anticipated having regard to the knowledge, oral or otherwise, available within any local or indigenous community in India or elsewhere".[4]

The Controller after hearing the parties takes a decision. If either party is not satisfied with the order of Controller of Patent, the aggrieved party may appeal to Intellectual Property Appellate Board (IPAB), Chennai against the order.

The ***fifth step*** is the grant and sealing of the patent. If the Controller is satisfied with the inventor's answer to the raised objections (if any), then patent is granted to the applicant under the seal of Patent Office. The details of patent along with the date on which it is sealed will be entered in the Register of patent office. This Register maintained in the Patent Office is an important legal document in case of patent disputes.

2.8 E-FILING OF PATENT APPLICATION

The Intellectual Property Office, India provides e-filing for enabling applicants to apply for a Patent online. It facilitates to complete an electronic application form, provides the associated attachments and completes the necessary payment details. The advantages of e-filing are that as anyone completes the application formalities online s/he receives a patent application number immediately. It speeds up the registration process, thus saving on time. The completed application data and fee acknowledgement may be saved on the PC or laptop and a printout may be taken for future reference.

The step-wise procedure for e-filing of patent is:

1. To acquire Class 3 Digital Signatures from either Tata Consultancy Services or (n)Code Solutions or Safe Script.
2. Use acquired Digital Signature details to get User ID and Password online from Indian Patent Office (IPO).

4. http://ipindia.nic.in/ipr/patent/patAct1970-3-99.html

3. Login using User ID and Password into the e-filing System of IPO.
4. Download the Client Software for preparing Patent Application Offline with required documents and Digitally Sign it for uploading on IPO Server.
5. Fill Patent Application offline and generate an XML file using Client Software.
6. Digitally Sign the completed application.
7. Login into e-patent portal (http://ipindia.gov.in) for uploading Application XML file on IPO Server.
8. Upload and submit Digitally Signed XML file to IPO server.
9. Process Application for EFT (Electronic Fund Transfer) using State Bank of India or Axis Bank Payment Gateways.
10. As EFT is completed, acknowledgement details will be displayed.
11. Click on 'Print' to take a printout of the acknowledgement receipt.
12. To confirm e-filing of the patent application, check the status of your Application. It will show list of all accepted patent applications that are submitted through e-filing. If your application reference number, address for correspondence, title of invention, date of filing appears with the status column showing ACCEPTED, then it is sure that the e-filing of patent application is complete.

The Patent Office in India plans to switch over to a completely paper-less office. The e-filing of patent application is a step in that direction.

2.9 TEMPORAL AND SPATIAL ASPECT OF PATENT

Each IPR has temporal and spatial aspects, i.e. its time and space parameters. The term of every patent is 20 years from the date of filing of patent application, irrespective of whether it is filed with provisional or complete specification. The date of the patent is the date on which the application for patent is filed. Regarding spatial aspects, the patent is a territorial right, i.e. it is valid only within the country in which it is granted. There is no term like 'world patent'. Examples are Indian Patent, US Patent and China Patent. However, patent applicant using a single application filled in any one approved language, may apply for patents at multiple signatory member countries as per PCT (Patent Cooperation Treaty) signed in 1970. Such patent applications are called PCT applications. India is signatory member of PCT.

2.10 OPPOSITION TO GRANT OF PATENT

In India, there is a provision for both pre-grant opposition and post-grant opposition. The pre-grant patent is within four months after the publication about the proposed patent in advertisement in the official Gazette. In case of post-grant opposition, anybody may file a written opposition within one year from the date of publication of grant of a patent in the Patent Office Journal. The grounds for opposition to the post-grant of patent are same as mentioned above in case of opposition to pre-grant patent. The patentee is given an opportunity to defend his/her case and give reply to the objections. A hearing of both the parties takes place and final decision is taken by the Controller.

2.11 RIGHTS OF PATENTEE

The Patent Act, 1970 and subsequent amendments in case of Product Patent provide patentee (patent holder/s) exclusive right to prevent others from performing, without authorization, the act of making, using, offering for sale, selling or importing that product for using or sale for 20 years from the date of grant of product patent.

In case of Process Patent, the Patent Act provides the patentee exclusive right to exclude others from performing, without his authorization, the act of using that process, using and offering for sale, selling or importing for those purposes, the product obtained directly by that process in India for 20 years from the date of grant of process patent.

2.12 PATENT OFFICE AND REGISTER OF PATENTS

The Patent office administers the various provisions of Patent Act, 1970 and subsequent amendments. The head office of Patents is at Kolkata. It has branch offices at Mumbai, Chennai and New Delhi. The Controller of Patents, Designs and Trade Mark is the Controller of Patents. The Patent Examiners are important personnel of the Patent office. Each Patent Examiner has own area of expertise and keeps him/her updated regarding inventions and developments in that particular field. The Patent Examiner does the three basic checks (as discussed above) to examine the patentability of the invention.

The Patent office also maintains Register of Patent, in which all particulars of the patentee, viz. the name and address of patentee, the title of the invention, the date of the patent, the date of sealing and the official number of the patent are mentioned. It also makes entry of assignment, transfers or revocation of patents, if any. It is an important legal document in the sense that in case of patent dispute this is taken as prima facie evidence admissible in the court of law. It is open to public inspection. In case of any error, it may be rectified only by the order of the Controller.

2.13 PCT PATENT

There is nothing like world patent, but the (signatory) member nations of Patent Cooperation Treaty (PCT) may file patent application in about 130 countries at one go, without having to file a separate application in all countries. This type of patent application is also called international application. It reduces the time and cost of obtaining patents in different countries. The applicant may choose one or more or all from these 130 countries. The fees will vary as per the number of countries any individual or organization is applying for patent under PCT. However, the actual power of grant of the patent remains with the concerned countries. India is a member of PCT since 7 December 1998. The members of PCT include major countries, like USA, France, UK, Japan and Germany. The PCT was signed on 19 June 1970, and came in force in 1978. All activities related to PCT are coordinated by the WIPO (World Intellectual Property Organization) situated in Geneva. The PCT had been amended from time-to-time to make it better suited as per the changing patent environment.

The international application filed through PCT system, where patent is to be applied at two or more countries, may be filed in any of the Branch Offices of the Patent Office at Kolkata, New Delhi, Chennai and Mumbai. That particular office shall function as Receiving Office (RO), designated office and elected office for the purpose of international applications filed under the treaty. Such nationals of member countries may file for an international search by International Search Authority (ISA). ISA would do a global search through its intensive database of patent literature of member nations available with them from 1920 till date. In case there is an adverse report by ISA, the PCT applicant may drop the application in one or more countries, thereby saving the time and fees involved. According to annual report released by Office of Controller General of Patents, Designs & Trade Marks for 2011–2012, 773 Indian applicants/legal entities filed international application using PCT system (Table 2.2).

In case of any clash, the national IPR law of a member nation prevails over PCT. The Indian Patent Act has similar conditions of patentability as PCT, except in case of micro-organisms. In India, the micro-organisms discovered from nature are not patentable. However, genetically modified micro-organisms are patentable.

Table 2.2 PCT International Application Filed by Indian Applicants

Year	*2005–06*	*2006–07*	*2007–08*	*2008–09*	*2009–10*	*2010–11*	*2011–12*
Individual	130	144	169	232	231	243	254
Legal entity	352	390	538	655	521	628	519
Total	482	534	707	887	752	871	773

Source: Annual Report, Office of Controller General of Patents, Designs, Trade Marks & Geographical Indications, India 2011–2012.

2.14 EXCLUSIVE MARKETING RIGHTS

As per TRIPS (Trade Related aspects of Intellectual Property Rights) Agreement, the countries not providing product patent in respect of drugs and agrochemical will have to provide Exclusive Marketing Rights (EMR) to the applicants if they "satisfy the following criteria:

(a) A patent application covering the new drug or agrochemical has been filed in any of the WTO member countries after 1 January 1995.
(b) A product patent should have been obtained in any of the member countries after 1 January 1995.
(c) Marketing approvals for the product has been obtained in any of the member countries.
(d) A patent application has already been filed after 1 January 1995 in the country where EMR is sought.
(e) The applicant should apply for EMR in the prescribed form and pay the requisite fee".[5]

The EMR is valid for five years or until the time the product patent law comes into effect. It gave rights only to sell the product, but not exclusive right to manufacture. In India the EMR came in effect from 26 March 1999, with the provision of retrospective effect from 1 January 1995. This provision was removed from Patent Act through an amendment in 2005, after which product patent regime came into force.

2.15 MILESTONES IN INDIAN PATENT LAW

The patent law in India was as per the country requirements before 1995. The Patent regulation environment started changing since 1 January 1995, when India became member of WTO. There were many advantages that accrued to Indian industry and citizens due to global integration through WTO. However, in terms of patents, it was loss for India in short-term, but was advantageous in the long run; given India's potential in innovation and research output. The Indian Amended Patent Act was rewarding for the organizations and individuals/groups that invested their resources in research and promoted innovation culture leading to product patents.

The process patent enabled cheaper medicine and other products in India before 1 January 1995. The cost of research of making the same product with a different process, i.e. cost of getting a 'process patent' was less, and hence, India benefitted from this type of patent regime. However, there was a growing pressure on India from developed nations through WTO to shift from 'process patent' to 'product patent' system. Earlier, India was supposed to be fully TRIPS compliant, i.e. including product patent by 2000. However, India took an extension from WTO for five more years so as to give more time to Indian organizations for better preparedness to TRIPS. India, as a part of its commitment to WTO, started EMR (Exclusive Marketing Rights) and mail box application facility for pharmaceutical and agrochemical products in

5. http://www.indianpatents.org.in

1995. As an amendment to Indian Patent Act of 1970, patent duration of all kinds of products was increased to 20 years in line with WTO norms, from earlier 14-year duration for most of the products. India implemented product patent for food, chemical and pharmaceutical on 1 January 2005; as a part of its commitment to WTO.

However, Indian government based on the experiences regarding product patents in other developed and developing countries and historical data had included many safeguards in Indian Amended Patent Act. For example, in case of public health emergency or security issues the government had power to revoke the patent or license it to third parties for mass production. It also made provisions for compulsory licensing so as to ensure availability of drugs at reasonable prices in the country. The 'reasonableness' of prices will be determined by the Indian government as per the Indian Amended Patent Act.

The agreement on TRIPS provides enough flexibility to the signatory member countries to interpret its own TRIPS obligation for implementation in their country. In case any organization is not satisfied even after court verdict challenging the patent office order, as was in the case of Swiss pharmaceutical company Novartis's anti-cancer drug Gleevec (refer Case Study at the end of this chapter), it may petition its national government to take the matter to WTO. If the Government is convinced with the organization plea about the TRIPS violation, it may lodge a formal complain at WTO's Dispute Settlement Board (DSB) against the other country.

2.16 SUMMARY

A patent is an intellectual property right relating to inventions and is the grant of exclusive right, for limited period, provided by the Government to the patentee, in exchange of full disclosure of his invention, for excluding others, from making, using, selling, importing the patented product or process producing that product for those purposes It may be filed individually or by two or more persons together or by any institution in order to protect their invention. The history of patent in India dates back to 19th century, when Britishers introduced the British Patent Law of 1852 in India. Over the period of time we have amended our laws many times to align fully with the TRIPS agreement of WTO, of which India is one of the signatory members.

The Patent for a product is granted on fulfilling the three important criteria, viz. novelty, non-obviousness and usefulness of the invention. There are certain inventions, like method of agriculture, surgical treatment of human beings, mathematical methods, etc. that are not patentable. There are two kinds of Patents—Product Patent for making a new product with a new process/method as compared to Process Patent in which an existing product is made by different method. Presently almost all member countries of WTO have Product Patent which is more comprehensive law for protection of invention against any kind of infringement.

The technical details of the invention/patented product are called specification. A provisional specification may be filed before complete specification in order to reserve his idea of invention. However, it cannot be reserved beyond twelve months in normal circumstances or maximum fifteen months in some special cases. The patent filing may be done through internet called e-filing or manually following certain procedures. The patent is granted for 20 years and is a territorial right, i.e. it is valid only in the country in which it is granted. In India, there is a provision for both pre-grant opposition and post-grant opposition of grant of patent.

There have been newer developments in the field of Patents. The PCT patent enables anybody to file patent in 130 countries through a single application form. This saves lot of time and money of the applicant. The countries not having the provision of product patent in particular category are required to offer Exclusive Marketing Rights (EMR) to the applicants in that category, till the product patent comes in effect. Also, the number of e-filing of patents is increasing which has resulted in expediting the process of submission, examination and grant of patent.

CASE STUDY—NOVARTIS IN INDIA

In early 2003, Swiss drug company Novartis AG launched its anti-cancer drug Gleevec in the US market, after obtaining it's US patent, at the rate of $2600 per patient per month. Soon in November 2003, Novartis launched Gleevec in India, by acquiring EMR (Exclusive Marketing Rights) as it saw India as a major revenue generating market for cancer drugs. At that time India did not provide product patent for medicines, and hence, EMR was only option for selling the drug in India. Gleevec was selling for $200 per patient per month in India. Novartis took legal recourse to stop other Indian drug manufacturers who were selling similar products with different brand names. In 2005, Madras High Court ordered Novartis to provide its anti-cancer drug Gleevec free to the patients who cannot afford it. The company reluctantly complied with the ruling. The Indian government asked Novartis to provide market-related data on the drug, the pricing and the number of patients who required it. The Government was planning to intervene, in the case, the price was too high or it was not being adequately distributed across the country. The options before the Government were either to license select domestic drug manufacturers to produce the same cancer drug or fix a reasonable price for Gleevec. Meanwhile the amendments to Indian Patent Act were passed in the parliament, which gave provision for grant of product patents for medicines in India. Novartis applied for Indian patent of its anti-cancer drug imatinib mesylate, which was marketed with the brand name of Gleevec. It could have given Novartis exclusive manufacturing and marketing rights of this anti-cancer drug in India for next 20 years. The patent application of Gleevec was rejected by Indian patent office in January 2006, citing Section 3(d). The Section 3(d) of amended Indian Patent Act stated that new forms of known substances will not qualify for patent. Section 3(d) was introduced to prevent evergreening of a patent. The patent office told Novartis that its anti-cancer drug imatinib mesylate (Gleevec) is simply a new form of known substance and did not show enhanced efficacy, and hence, it cannot qualify to get an Indian patent. Novartis took it as a setback to its planned revenue growth in India. In May 2006, it challenged the validity of Section 3(d) of amended Indian Patent Act in High Court of Madras (Chennai). The High Court of Madras on 6 August 2007, in its final ruling, rejected Novartis claim citing Section 3(d) of the Indian Amended Patent Act as constitutional. As a reaction Novartis AG put on hold new investments in India citing lack of clarity on IPR issues in India.

ISSUES FOR DISCUSSION

1. Comment on the economic impact in terms of FDI (Foreign Direct Investment) especially in pharmaceutical sector, in case the government intervenes by way of price fixation for Gleevec or licenses it for mass production to local manufacturers?
2. What is the rationale behind Section 3(d) of amended Indian Patent Act? How was it related to evergreening of a patent?
3. Differentiate between EMR and product patent by taking Gleevec as an example.
4. What steps Novartis AG took after the Madras High Court judgement? Did Switzerland file a case in WTO's DSB (Dispute Settlement Board) against India in the Novartis case? If not, what may be the reasons behind this decision?

Discussion Questions

1. Define Patent. Elaborate the conditions for the grant of Patent.
2. What do mean by Product Patent and Process Patent? Differentiate between the two.
3. 'There are certain inventions which are not patentable as per the Patent Act, 1970 and subsequent amendments'. Comment on the validity of the statement and enumerate the inventions not patentable, if any.
4. Discuss in detail the procedure for the grant of patent.
5. How e-filing of Patents is done in India? Elaborate the procedure.
6. What do you mean by specification? Differentiate between provisional specification and complete specification.
7. What is EMR? What are criteria for granting EMR for a product?
8. What are the grounds on which the granting of a patent may be opposed?
9. What is PCT patent? What is procedure for applying PCT patent in India?

10. Write short notes on:
    (a) Rights of Patentee
    (b) Register of Patents
11. Discuss briefly the history of Patents in India.
12. What are temporal and spatial aspects of Patents?

Objective Type Questions

Tick the right answer in given multiple-choice questions:

1. The Head office of Patents is at
   (a) New Delhi (b) Kolkata (c) Chennai (d) Mumbai
2. The Patent is granted for
   (a) 10 years (b) 15 years (c) 20 years (d) 25 years
3. The Patent granted in India is applicable
   (a) All over the world
   (b) India only
   (c) India and China
   (d) India and USA
4. Which of the following is not an essential condition for grant of patent
   (a) Design (b) Novelty (c) Non-Obvious (d) Useful
5. The technical description of a patent is called
   (a) Detail (b) Specification (c) EMR (d) Design
6. Which of the following is not patentable
   (a) Drug (b) Microprocessor
   (c) I-pod (d) Mathematical Method
7. The Branch office of Patents is not located at
   (a) New Delhi (b) Allahabad (c) Mumbai (d) Chennai
8. Complete Specification has to be submitted after filing provisional specification within a period of
   (a) 6 months (b) 12 months (c) 24 months (d) 18 months
9. Indian Patent Act provides .... in case of grant of patent.
   (a) Pre-grant Opposition (b) Post-grant Opposition
   (c) Both pre-grant and post-grant opposition
   (d) None of these
10. In case of opposition hearing for grant of patent, whose decision is final
    (a) Controller (b) Patent Examiner
    (c) Deputy-Controller (d) Director

Mark TRUE or FALSE against given statements:

1. The patent provides an exclusive legal right for an infinite period to the inventor. (True/False)
2. There is no such thing like world patent. (True/False)
3. Process Patent is same product, different process whereas Product Patent is different product, different process. (True/False)
4. Inventions relating to atomic energy are patentable in India. (True/False)
5. All activities related to PCT are coordinated by the WIPO (World Intellectual Property Organization) situated in Geneva. (True/False)

References

Annual Report, Office of Controller General of Patents, Designs, Trade Marks & Geographical Indications, India 2009–10, Department of Industrial Policy and Promotion, Ministry of Commerce and Industry, Government of India; Available at http://ipindia.gov.in/cgpdtm/AnnualReport_English_2009_2010.pdf

Annual Report, Office of Controller General of Patents, Designs, Trade Marks & Geographical Indications, India 2010–11, Department of Industrial Policy and Promotion, Ministry of Commerce and Industry, Government of India; Available at http://ipindia.nic.in/cgpdtm/AnnualReport_English_2010_2011.pdf

Annual Report, Office of Controller General of Patents, Designs, Trade Marks & Geographical Indications, India 2011–12, Department of Industrial Policy and Promotion, Ministry of Commerce and Industry, Government of India; Available at http://ipindia.gov.in/cgpdtm/AnnualReport_English_2011_2012.pdf

Forms and Fees for Patent Filing in India, Patent Information Centre, Punjab State Council for Science & Technology, Chandigarh

Geetika and Pandey, Neeraj (2004), "Intellectual Property and Technological Developments: Changing Dynamics and Newer Perspectives," *Proceedings of the National Seminar on Intellectual Property Rights*; pp. 170–178.

Hidalgo, Antonio (2009), "Analysis of the Commercial Use of Spanish Inventions protected by Patents between 1996 and 2006", *Journal of Intellectual Property Rights*, Volume 14, pp. 63–69.

Kardam, K.S. (2007), "Patenting in the Emerging Fields of Technology", *Journal of Intellectual Property Rights*, Volume 13, pp. 15–29.

Narayanan, P., *Intellectual Property Law*, Eastern Law House, Kolkata, 2001.

Nagori, B.P. and Mathur, Vipin (2009), "Basics of Writing Patent Non-Infringement and Freedom-to-Operate Opinions", *Journal of Intellectual Property Rights*, Volume 14, pp. 7–13.

Pandey, Neeraj and Bhattacharya, K.K. (2008), "The Academia Dynamics in New Intellectual Property Regime in Third World Countries", *Journal of the World Universities Forum*, Volume 1, Number 2, pp. 1–7.

Rines, Robert H. (2007), "Should India and other countries adopt the American 'Business Methods' class of Patents", *Journal of Intellectual Property Rights*, Volume 12, pp. 183–184.

Some Questions and Answers on Patents, Copyrights, Designs, Trademarks, IC Layout Designs, Geographical Indications, Patent Facilitating Centre, TIFAC, New Delhi, 2005.

Sheehe, Johanna (2009), "Indian Patent law: Walking the Line?", *Northwestern Journal of International Law & Business*, Volume 29, pp. 577–599.

The Patent Act, 1970 Bare Acts, Universal Law Publishing, 2010.

Thomas, Zakir (2008), "IP Case Law Developments", *Journal of Intellectual Property Rights*, Volume 13, pp. 157–164.

Websites

http://ipsnews.net/news.asp?idnews=35348

http://www.ipindia.nic.in

http://ipindia.nic.in/ipr/patent/patents_filing.pdf

http://www.wipo.int

CHAPTER 3

Transfer and Infringement of Patent Rights

Patent is a territorial right which may be commercialized by the patent holder or it may be licensed to a third party for manufacturing/marketing or may be altogether sold or gifted to the third party depending on the prerogative of the patent holder. Patent is considered as strongest form of intellectual property protection against any kind of infringement. This is the reason why many of the IT companies, who were traditionally getting copyright for the software, are now trying to get patent for newly developed software. The Indian Patent Office provides several safeguards against any infringement of patent rights of the patentee.

3.1 TRANSFER OF PATENT RIGHTS

The transfer of patent rights is done either by assignment of patent or by licence. Assignment of patent involves complete transfer of patent to the assignee (person/entity to whom it is transferred) by the assignor (the original patent holder who transferred the patent). The transfer of patent rights by licence involves conferring of specific patent rights in parts or as a whole to the third party. In transfer through assignment the name of assignee is registered in the Register of Patent (a legal document) kept with Controller of Patent's office, whereas in Licence it is not so.

3.1.1 Assignment

Section 68 of the Patent Act, 1970 provides for assignment and licence of patent rights. There are three types of assignment of patent:

(a) Legal Assignment

Legal Assignment is the best form of patent transfer from the assignee perspective. It involves complete transfer of patent rights from the assignor (original patent holder) to the assignee. The name of assignee is entered in the Register of patents kept with the Controller of Patent's office as proprietor of the patent. The assignee enjoys all rights as original patent holder.

(b) Equitable Assignment

This is another form of assignment of patent rights in which assignee is granted certain defined rights as per the agreement between assignor and the assignee. A document regarding this agreement is registered in the Controller of Patent's office. However, the name of the assignee in the case of equitable assignment of patent transfer is not entered in the Register of patents as proprietor.

(c) Mortgage

Another method of transfer of patent under assignment is the mortgage of patent to a third party against certain mutually agreed sum of money. The name of the third party is entered in Register of patents as mortgagee. When the original patent holder returns the sum of money as per the agreement the patent is re-transferred to his name and name of third party as mortgagee is struck off the Register of patents.

3.1.2 Licence

There are two main types of transfer of patent through licence:

(a) Voluntary Licence

As the name suggests, the patent holder provides licence voluntarily to the third party through a written agreement to manufacture or market on mutually agreed terms and conditions. The Controller of patents is informed within six months of agreement. However the Controller has no role to play in case of voluntary licence.

(b) Compulsory Licence

Compulsory licence is granted by the Controller of patents in exceptional cases. It is a safeguard mechanism embedded in the TRIPS (Trade Related Intellectual Property Rights) agreement of WTO to take care of extraordinary market conditions. Under compulsory licence, the Controller of patents after expiry of 3 years of grant of patent, on an application, may grant compulsory licence to a third party, "on any of following grounds:

- The reasonable requirements of public with respect to the patented invention had not been satisfied, or
- The patented invention is not available to the public at a reasonably affordable price, or
- The patented invention is not worked in the territory of India".[1]

1. http://www.patentoffice.nic.in/ipr/patent/ipti/Topic%205.ppt

The reasonableness would be decided by Controller of patents.

Also, Section 97 of The Patent Act, 1970, states that Government of India through the official Gazette may provide compulsory licensing of any product at any time after sealing of such patent if it becomes necessary in the public interest.

3.2 INFRINGEMENT OF PATENT RIGHTS

A patent holder has the sole right for manufacturing, marketing and distribution of the invented product. In case any third party who is using the same product by way of manufacturing, marketing and distribution without the patent holder permission amounts to infringement of the patent. Chapter XVIII of The Patent Act, 1970 clearly delineates the conditions for infringement of the patent. They are:

(a) Colorable Imitations of any technical feature of the invention
(b) Immaterial variations in the invention
(c) Mechanical equivalents of any technical feature of the invention
(d) Consideration of essential features of the invention

Many of above conditions would overlap during infringement of patent. The colorable imitation and immaterial variation amount to cosmetic changes in an existing product or process to pass it as innovative new product. For example, mere changing the position of sub-parts of machinery or changing the exterior look of a product will not amount to novelty. Similarly, mechanical equivalents amount to using substitute parts in invention by the third party for getting same result for the same process. The essential features of the invention amount to using the core technology/process of the patentee and only changing the peripheral processes to claim novelty. Occasionally, such infringement is not proved in a court of law as the essential features of invention have not been properly claimed by the patentee at the time of filing patent application. Such patent are weak and susceptible to infringement.

The construction of claim by the patent attorney or the applicant should cover each and every aspect of the invention in the patent application. This helps in securing the patent more strongly against possible infringements.

However, certain acts (given below) "are not considered as infringement of patent:

- Any act of making or constructing including using, selling or importing a patented invention solely for uses reasonably related to the development and submission of information required under any law in the country.
- Importation of patented products by any person from a person who is duly authorized through assignment or licence".[2]

2. http://www.patentoffice.nic.in

3.3 DOCTRINE OF PITH AND MARROW

The doctrine of Pith and Marrow states that when deciding about infringement of a patent, it should be considered whether the essence of the invention has been infringed. Hence, even if any entity has cleverly violated someone's patent by using some loophole in the law but in essence it is an infringement, the court may use doctrine of Pith and Marrow to pronounce the judgement that there has been an infringement. For example, in an infringement dispute between Bajaj Auto Limited and TVS Motor Company, the Madras High Court used doctrine of Pith and Marrow to grant interim injunction on TVS from manufacturing, marketing, selling and exporting two or three wheelers with an internal combustion engine, including the new TVS Flame 125 cc or any such engine or product which infringes on Bajaj's patent (refer complete case at end of the chapter).

3.4 REMEDIES

The Patent Act, 1970 and its subsequent amendments, including The Patent Rules, 2003 and Patent (Amendment) Rules, 2006 provides remedies against any kind of infringement of patent rights of the patentee. Section 104 of The Patent Act, 1970, states that infringement proceeding would be initiated in a District Court or any higher court as per the area of jurisdiction. However, a counter-claim for revocation of the patent the case, along with the counter-claim, shall be transferred to the High Court for decision. The responsibility to establish infringement is on the plaintiff who filed the case. The time limit for filing the case against infringement is three years from the date of infringement. Section 108 of The Patent Act, 1970, provides following remedies against infringement of patent:

(a) Injunction

The injunction ruling by the court ensures that the infringement is stopped as and where it is and thus, prevents any future loss to the plaintiff. The injunction may be interim (temporary) or permanent. The interim injunction is granted early during the court proceedings on initial evidence to avoid further damage during pendency of the trial. In case the plaintiff wins the case, the interim injunction is converted into permanent.

(b) Damages or an Account of Profits

The court on culmination of trial may award damages or an account of profits to the winning plaintiff. Damages may be any amount that the court deems fit as the compensation for amount lost or injury suffered by the plaintiff due to the infringement of patent. An account of profits includes a share or the total profit earned due to the infringement by the infringer of the patent.

However, in certain cases, the damages or an account of profits cannot be granted. Such exceptions are:

- The defendant was not aware and had no reasonable grounds for believing that the patent existed.
- The infringement was committed after a failure to pay any renewal fee by the plaintiff within the prescribed period and before any extension of that period.
- The specification was amended and infringement was committed before the date of the decision allowing the amendment; unless the court is satisfied that the specification as originally published was framed in good faith and with reasonable skill and knowledge.

Section 108 of The Patent Act, 1970 states that either damages or an account of profits be compensated to the plaintiff, but both reliefs cannot be granted together.

3.5 PATENT AGENTS

All eligible patent agents are required to register their names in the 'Register of patent agents' maintained by the Controller of patents. In India 'patent agent' is same as 'patent attorney' in western countries. The qualification for being a patent agent is:

- A citizen of India
- Completed 21 years of age
- Graduate in science, engineering or technology
- Passes the qualifying examination prescribed for the purpose; or is an advocate; or served as a patent examiner or Controller for not less than 10 years
- Paid the prescribed fee

The Office of Controller General of Patents, Designs, Trade Marks & Geographical Indications has constituted Patent Agent Examination Board (PAEB) so as to enhance the credibility and transparency in Patent Agent examination. The academicians and experienced Patent Agents are part of PAEB besides senior officials of Indian patent office.

3.5.1 Right of Patent Agents

Every patent agent whose name is entered in the register is entitled:

- To practice before the Controller;
- To prepare all documents, transact all business and discharge of such other functions as may be prescribed in connection with any proceedings before the Controller.

3.6 SURRENDER OF PATENTS

A patentee may surrender the patent any time by giving notice to the Controller. The Controller publishes the offer in the prescribed format and notifies every person other than the patentee whose name appears in the register as having interest in the patent. Any interested party may raise objection to the Controller within the prescribed period. The Controller would forward the objection to the patentee for reply. If the Controller is satisfied after hearing the patentee and hearing of opponents, the patent may be surrendered. The Controller would by order revoke the patent.

3.7 BUDAPEST TREATY FOR PATENTS IN MICROBIOLOGICAL INVENTIONS

Budapest Treaty is an international convention governing the recognition of deposits in officially approved culture collections for the purpose of patent applications in any country that is signatory to the convention. The Treaty was signed in Budapest in 1973 and later amended in the year 1980. India joined the Budapest Treaty for patents in microbiological inventions on 17 December 2001. It is compulsory for the inventor to deposit a strain in any of the designated culture collection centre for testing; and examination by other member countries, in case they feel so. The culture collection becomes necessary as it is not possible to reproduce a microorganism from the limited description of it in a patent specification. The culture collection centre allocates a registration number to the deposited microorganism. Thus, inventor need not give complete specification of the invention, which further protects any kind of infringement. The allocated registration number by the culture collection centre is to be quoted in the patent application. Anyone wanting to do further research using the microorganism may do so by procuring it from the designated culture collection centre.

3.8 CHALLENGES IN PATENTS

As filing and grant of patent increased over the years, new challenges have emerged in the patent arena. The important issues in patents include:

3.8.1 Evergreening of Patent

The patent rights are valid for 20 years. After the expiry of this period, the invention becomes the part of public knowledge which may be manufactured and sold in the open market by various companies or it may be used for further innovation to invent new products. However, many of drug manufacturers extend their patent by again getting the similar generic patent either by slightly changing method of treatment, mechanism of action, derivatives, isomeric forms, dosing regimen, delivery profiles, etc. Thus, the patent holder companies resort to patent term extension strategies by infusing cosmetic novelty—which many a times are just new forms of already patented generic drug (of which patent is about to expire). As a result the price of such products does not come down and it facilitates monopoly and inhibits innovation. The Indian Patent Act discourages evergreening of the patents. Section 3(d) of Patent Act, 1970 states that patent will not be granted for "the mere discovery of a new form of a known substance which does not result in the enhancement of the known efficacy of that substance or the mere discovery of any new property or new use for a known substance or of the mere new use of a known process, machine or apparatus unless such known process results in a new product or employs at least one new reactant".[3]

3.8.2 Funding Issues

Apart from funding support required for facilitating innovation and patent culture, the issue of patent rights is also important especially in cases of sponsored research. The Indian Government is bringing legislation similar to Bayh-Dole Act of USA which provides the individuals and universities the right to patent discoveries in their name resulting from federally funded research and also generate revenue by commercializing, licensing or selling it to third party. This will help in motivating scientists, academicians and practitioners for research and generating patents by leveraging government funding and getting engaged in public-private partnership funded research.

3.8.3 Increasing Commercial Patents

The patent data shows that less than two percent of patents are commercialized globally. It means the innovations are not being used for mass production and not being used by the public at large. The reasons *inter alia* may be high prototype cost, incremental innovation not adding enough value to the end customer, academic purposes only, lack of awareness about commercialization, lack of government facilitation and lack of incentive for undertaking commercialization. This phenomenon does not augur well for innovation and society at large. In order to complete this value chain of innovation by way of commercialization more public-private partnership should be promoted by the government. Incentives in the form of certain tax exemptions, easy credit facilities, infrastructural support, like incubation for commercialization of patents, etc. would help in arresting this negative trend.

3. http://indianpatent.com/pages/faq_patent.htm

3.8.4 Awareness Issue

The lack of awareness about patents and its related advantages to an individual or organization is one of the most important reasons for low patenting activity from a billion plus nation. Indians have traditionally known to be innovative and ingenious, but the majority of rural India does not know anything about patent. Organizations, like SRISTI (Society for Research and Initiatives for Sustainable Technologies and Institutions), GIAN (Grassroots Innovation Augmentation Network) and NIF (National Innovation Foundation) are helping rural innovators to patent their products and facilitating commercialization of these products. Many of innovations are not reported and filed for patent due to lack of proper awareness. Novel ideas, at times, due to lack of awareness are discussed at public forums or published before filing for patents; thus losing the 'novelty'. Many of the researchers do not know how to file a patent or whom to contact for filing a patent. Training and creating awareness about various facets of patents has been consistently taken up by the Indian government through its various Patent Information Centers to bridge this gap.

3.8.5 Delay in Grant of Patent

The Indian patent office takes, on an average, more than two years to grant a patent since the date of filing the patent application. In majority of the cases it takes about three to four years in final grant and sealing of the patent. The time taken for processing of patent applications is much higher as compared to international standards. This causes dissatisfaction amongst the inventor organization/individual besides becoming inhibiting factor in attracting research and development talent and investment in the country. The main reason behind this delay in application processing and grant of patent application is lesser number of Patent Examiner in the Indian patent office and increased number of patent application filings in India (Table 3.1). This had increased work load on the Patent Examiners multifold.

Table 3.1 Filing and Grant of Patents in India

Year	*2003–2004*	*2004–2005*	*2005–2006*	*2006–2007*	*2007–2008*	*2008–2009*	*2009–2010*	*2010–2011*	*2011–2012*
Filed	12613	17466	24505	28940	35218	36812	34287	39400	43197
Examined	10709	14813	11569	14119	11751	10296	6069	11208	11031
Granted	2469	1911	4320	7539	15316	16061	6430	7509	4381

Source: Annual Report, Office of Controller General of Patents, Designs, Trade Marks & Geographical Indications, India 2009–2010; 2010–2011 and 2011–2012.

According to annual report released by Office of Controller General of Patents, Designs & Trade Marks for 2009–2010, there was high attrition of Patent Examiners. About 55 Patent Examiners resigned during 2004–2009, and no new recruitments took place during this period. Also, 47 Patent Examiners were promoted as Assistant Controllers in January, 2009; thus further decreasing the main patent processing frontline workforce of Indian patent office. These development lead to lesser number of patent examination and grant in 2009–2010. The Controller General of Patents, Designs & Trade Marks had taken a series of step to streamline the patent processing in India. It included recruitment of sufficient number of patent Examiners, digitization of records, complete electronic processing of patent applications and increased accountability of patent Examiners and Assistant Controllers. The patent office had also outsourced some of its non-core activities so as to further expedite the processing of patent applications.

3.8.6 Balancing Competition and Cooperation

The patent culture has brought a cut throat competitive environment not only in the industry but also in academia and research institutions. Since there are commercial issues involved, generally the research is pursued in secretive and closed environment to maintain idea uniqueness till the patent is filed. The open knowledge sharing culture and cooperation across individuals, groups and organizations becomes a central issue in such a hyper competitive patent-oriented environment. Many-a-times, organizations, groups or individuals try to maintain their dominance by not sharing any information to other innovators who are developing advanced research products using the patented technologies or tests. Evergreening is also one of the strategies to unduly maintain their commercial dominance. Also there are frivolous cases of patent infringement against individuals and enterprises involved in research of competing and superior technologies by the rivals. Such approaches hamper the innovation culture, and thereby using patents negatively to gain competitive advantage. The patenting policy of the respective nations should ensure that there exists a healthy patenting environment for a sustainable economic future of the nation.

3.8.7 Cost of Patent Services

The cost of patenting is high in most of the countries including the PCT international patent filing fee. The cost of patenting includes not only the patent application fee but also the patent attorney/agent fee, and regular patent maintenance fee during the 20-year duration of patent. There are other cost implications, like translation fee if one has to get the patent document translated in other native language. Also in case the patent document has beyond certain number of pages, there is extra charge per page. The services of patent attorney/agent are optional. However, it is advisable to take profession services of patent attorney/agent, especially if anyone is filing patent for the first time. The patent attorney/agent helps in securing the patent by technically elaborating the patent besides helping in application processing and resolving objections from the patent office, if any. In India the cost of filing patent is reasonable. It is about thirty five hundred rupees (₹3500). The cost of patenting increases in cases of objections raised by third party against the field patent, if any. The fees of the patent attorney/agent, court fee, appeal fee, etc. enhance the overall liability in such cases.

3.9 SUMMARY

Patent is the strongest of all IPRs in terms of security against infringement. Since patent is like a legal property it may be gifted, transferred, mortgaged or licensed for specific activities to a third party, solely based on the prerogative of the patentee. The best form of transfer of patent rights, from the third party perspective, is the legal assignment of patent. In this assignment, the name of the assignee is entered in the Register of patents. The assignee in legal assignment has similar rights as the original patent holder. The Register of patents is a legal document, maintained by Controller of patents. Other forms of assignment of patent are equitable assignment and mortgage. Transfer by Licence includes voluntary and compulsory licence. Compulsory licence is granted sparingly in case of extraordinary requirement as per Section 97 of The Patent Act. Colorable imitations of the invention, immaterial variations, mechanical equivalents of any technical feature of the invention and using essential features of the invention amount to infringement of patent. The Patent Act provides relief in case of any infringement. The court may order injunction on the basis of prima facie evidence to avoid further damage during pendency of the trial. In case the plaintiff wins the case, the interim injunction is converted into permanent. The court may also allow either a certain amount of damage as it deems fit or an account of profits as compensation for amount lost or injury suffered by the plaintiff due to the infringement of patent. Patent agents are an important link between plaintiff and the Controller of patents for presenting their case. Evergreening of patent, funding, increasing commercial patents and enhancing awareness regarding patent among masses are major emerging challenges in the patent arena.

CASE STUDY—BAJAJ AUTO LIMITED VS. TVS MOTOR COMPANY

The Madras High Court on 16 February 2008 restrained TVS—the third largest two wheeler company—from manufacturing, marketing, selling and exporting two or three wheelers with an internal combustion engine, including the new TVS Flame 125 cc or any such engine or product which infringes on Bajaj's patent. The interim injunction came after Pune based Bajaj Auto Limited—the second largest two wheeler company, approached Madras High Court charging Chennai based TVS Motor Company of infringing on its digital twin spark ignition (DTSi) technology while using controlled combustion variable intelligent technology (CCVTi) in TVS new 125 cc 'Flame' bike. However, after complete hearing of the case for more than a year, the Madras High Court on 19 May 2009 set aside its own order and allowed TVS Motor Company for manufacturing and marketing vehicles with twin spark technology. The official statement from TVS Motor Company is that the patent granted to Bajaj Auto is for 'ExhausTEC', which is a chamber fitted on the exhaust pipe and it has nothing to do with 'DTSi twin spark' technology. DTSi technology involves the use of two spark plugs in the cylinder head, which is part of the engine. 'ExhausTEC' is not fitted on the engine, but is fitted in the exhaust pipe and refers to an additional chamber which is created in the exhaust pipe through which exhaust gases are dispensed. As per TVS perspective, these are two separate patents and are not linked to each other. Bajaj Auto had been using the twin spark technology in all of ten models since more than five years. This way Bajaj had already gained the first mover advantage. Bajaj Auto challenged the Madras High Court order in Supreme Court through Special Leave Petition. After hearing both the parties, Supreme Court on 16 September 2009 held that TVS was free to sell its product "Flame" with twin spark technology. The Supreme Court also directed TVS to maintain and file accounts of sales. The Supreme Court ordered that the suit before the Madras High Court should be heard on a day-to-day basis and that the hearing be concluded by 30 November 2009.

ISSUES FOR DISCUSSION

1. Discuss the interim and permanent injunction as a remedy to infringement, taking examples from the case.
2. What were advantages of interim injunction to the plaintiff, i.e. Bajaj Auto Limited?
3. In the light of facts in the case, analyze the future strategy of TVS Motor Company.
4. Track the developments post 30 November 2009 Madras High Court ruling and status of technology used in TVS and Bajaj Auto products post the final judgement.

Discussion Questions

1. Enumerate the various methods for transfer of patents as per The Patent Act, 1970.
2. What are various types of assignment of patent?
3. Differentiate between legal assignment and equitable assignment.
4. What is compulsory licensing?
5. Differentiate between voluntary licensing and compulsory licensing.
6. What amounts to infringement of patents? Discuss the remedies granted under The Patent Act, 1970 for infringement of patent.
7. What are the eligibility criteria for becoming a patent agent?

8. Discuss, in brief, the reasons behind low percentage of commercialization of patent.
9. What do you mean by injunction of patent?
10. What is evergreening of patents? What is the impact of evergreening of patents?

Objective Type Questions

Tick the right answer in given multiple-choice questions:

1. Patent cannot be transferred by
   (a) Assignment (b) Request (c) Licence (d) Mortgage
2. The best form of transfer through assignment, from the assignee perspective, is
   (a) Legal (b) Equitable (c) Mortgage (d) Voluntary
3. The name of the assignee is registered in Register of Patent in
   (a) Legal Assignment (b) Equitable Assignment
   (c) Mortgage (d) Voluntary Licence
4. An application for compulsory licence may be filled with Controller after expiry of how many years of grant of patent
   (a) 1 year (b) 2 years (c) 3 years (d) 4 years
5. A patent agent should have minimum age of
   (a) 18 years (b) 20 years (c) 21 years (d) 30 years
6. .... is strongest of all IPRs in terms of security against infringement.
   (a) Copyright (b) Trade Secrets (c) Patent (d) Trade Mark
7. The court may order .... on the basis of prima facie evidence to avoid further damage during pendency of the trial.
   (a) Injunction (b) Damages (c) An account of profit
   (d) None of them
8. The phenomenon of extending the patent before the expiry by resorting to cosmetic novelty or superficial change in generic patented product is called
   (a) Sealing (b) Commercial (c) Evergreening (d) Infringement
9. .... are an important link between plaintiff and the Controller of patents for presenting the patent case.
   (a) Controller (b) Patent examiner
   (c) Deputy-Controller (d) Patent agent
10. Register of patents is maintained by
    (a) Controller (b) Patent agent (c) Attorney (d) Plaintiff

Mark TRUE or FALSE against given statements:

1. In case of infringement, the court may either grant damages or an account of profits be compensated to the plaintiff, but both reliefs cannot be granted together. (True / False)
2. Section 111 of the Patent Act, 1970 provides for assignment and licence of patent rights. (True / False)
3. The name of the assignee in the case of equitable assignment of patent transfer is not entered in the Register of patents as proprietor. (True / False)
4. The infringement proceeding are initiated in court lower than District Court. (True / False)
5. All eligible patent agents are required to register their names in the 'Register of patent agents' maintained by the Controller of patents. (True / False)

References

Annual Report, Office of Controller General of Patents, Designs, Trade Marks & Geographical Indications, India 2009-10, Department of Industrial Policy and Promotion, Ministry of Commerce and Industry, Government of India; Available at http://ipindia.gov.in/cgpdtm/AnnualReport_English_2009_2010.pdf

Annual Report, Office of Controller General of Patents, Designs, Trade Marks & Geographical Indications, India 2010-11, Department of Industrial Policy and Promotion, Ministry of Commerce and Industry, Government of India; Available at http://ipindia.nic.in/cgpdtm/AnnualReport_English_2010_2011.pdf

Annual Report, Office of Controller General of Patents, Designs, Trade Marks & Geographical Indications, India 2011-12, Department of Industrial Policy and Promotion, Ministry of Commerce and Industry, Government of India; Available at http://ipindia.gov.in/cgpdtm/AnnualReport_English_2011_2012.pdf

Bansal, Inderjit Singh; Sahu, Deeptymaya, Bakshi, Gautam and Singh, Sukhjeet (2009), "Evergreening—A Controversial Issue in Pharma Milieu", *Journal of Intellectual Property Rights*, Volume 14, pp. 299–306.

Field, Thomas G. Jr. (2007), "Patent Systems: More Easily Faulted Than Fixed", *Journal of Intellectual Property Rights*, Volume 14, pp. 129–141.

Geetika and Pandey, Neeraj (2004), "Intellectual Property and Technological Developments: Changing Dynamics and Newer Perspectives", *Proceedings of the National Seminar on Intellectual Property Rights*; pp. 170–178.

Kochupillai, Mrinalini and Smith, Matthew A. (2007), "Patent Valuation with Consideration for Emerging Technologies", *Journal of Intellectual Property Rights*, Volume 12, pp. 154–164.

Pandey, Neeraj and Bhattacharya, K.K. (2008), "The Academia Dynamics in New Intellectual Property Regime in Third World Countries" *Journal of the World Universities Forum*, Volume 1, Number 2, pp. 1–7.

Some Questions and Answers on Patents, Copyrights, Designs, Trademarks, IC Layout Designs, Geographical Indications, Patent Facilitating Centre, TIFAC, New Delhi, 2005.

The Patent Act, 1970 Bare Acts, Universal Law Publishing, 2010.

Wadhera, B.L., *Laws Relating to Patents*, Trade Marks, Copyright, Designs & Geographical Indications, Universal Law Publishing, Delhi, 2002.

Websites

http://www.business-standard.com/india/news/madras-hc-allows-tvs-to-use-bajaj%5Cs-patented-tech/358569/

http://www.indianpatent.com/pages/faq_patent.htm

http://www.ipindia.nic.in

http://www.ipindia.nic.in/ipr/patent/patAct1970-3-99.html

http://www.patentoffice.nic.in/ipr/patent/ipti/Topic%205.ppt

http://www.wipo.int

CHAPTER 4

Copyright

The copyright was originally started by government machinery to restrict public from publishing certain documents. Later, this right was formally extended to individuals, public and private entities to use it to protect their documented intellectual property and utilize it commercially. Along with Patent, this is most popular intellectual property right. Generally, copyright extends beyond the lifetime of the creator making it attractive propositions for authors, programmers, musicians, artists, film directors, etc. to go for the copyright of their creation. The unique aspect of this intellectual property is that any document becomes a copyright the moment it is created. However, the onus of the proof lies with the original creator in case of disputes to prove that s/he was the first creator of that particular piece of work.

The copyright issues in India are governed by The Copyright Act, 1957 which was amended in 1983, 1984, 1992, 1994 and 1999. The copyright laws in India were amended in order to bring it in conformity with the international conventions, like TRIPs, Berne Convention and Universal Copyright Convention. Copyright, along with Trade Marks, are the most sensitive of all IPRs. Their infringement is quite easy due to gadgets, like photocopier, pendrive, tape recorder, video cassette recorder and ipods. The infringement of copyright and trade mark attract criminal suit to deter their violation. The copyright is unique among all IPRs because it is almost universally applicable without applying for copyright in each and every country like patent and trade mark. Under the Copyright Act, 1957 ideas are not subject to copyright, whereas the expression of the idea, in document form, is subject matter of copyright.

4.1 WHAT IS COPYRIGHT?

Copyright provides protection to the expression of the idea as envisaged under the Copyright Act, 1957. As per Section 13 of The Copyright Act, 1957 "the copyright subsist in the following classes of work:

- Literary works
- Dramatic works

- Musical works
- Artistic works
- Cinematograph films; and
- Sound Recording

4.1.1 Literary Works

Literary works include computer programs, tables and compilations including computer databases. Computer program means a set of instructions expressed in words, codes, schemes or in any other form, including a machine readable medium, capable of causing a computer to perform a particular task or achieve a particular result.

4.1.2 Dramatic Works

Dramatic works include any piece of recitation, choreographic work or entertainment in dumb show, the scenic arrangement or acting, form of which is fixed in writing or otherwise but does not include a cinematograph film.

4.1.3 Musical Works

Musical works include a work consisting of music, and includes any graphical notation of such work, but does not include any words or any action intended to be sung, spoken or performed with music.

4.1.4 Artistic Works

Artistic works include a painting; a sculpture; a drawing including a diagram, map, chart or plan; an engraving or a photograph and any other work of artistic craftsmanship.

4.1.5 Cinematograph Films

Cinematograph films include any work of visual recording on any medium produced through a process from which a moving image may be produced by any means and includes a sound recording accompanying such visual recording. It also includes video films.

4.1.6 Sound Recording

Sound Recording includes recording of sounds from which such sounds may be produced regardless of medium and method by which sounds were produced".[1]

---

1. http://copyright.gov.in

4.2 MEANING OF PUBLICATION

The meaning of publication as per The Copyright Act, 1957 is making a work available to the public by issue of copies, or by communicating the work to the public. However, in case of infringement of copyright, the work will not be deemed to be published. Section 5 of The Copyright Act, 1957 states that in case a work is published simultaneously—one in India and other abroad, the work published in India shall be deemed to be first published in India; unless the other country provides a shorter term of copyright for such work and the gap of publication date between the two countries is less than thirty days.

4.3 COPYRIGHT OFFICE AND COPYRIGHT BOARD

The Copyright Act, 1957 and its subsequent amendments provide for copyright office under the control of Registrar of Copyrights, who shall act under the superintendence and direction of the central government. The copyright office has a seal of its own. The Deputy Registrar of Copyrights, section officers and examiners assist the Registrar of Copyrights for the smooth functioning of the organization (Figure 4.1).

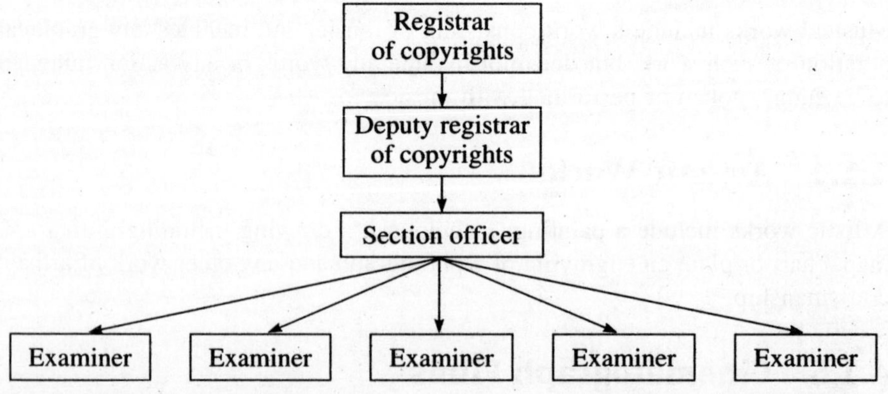

Source: http://copyright.gov.in

Figure 4.1 Organization Structure of Copyright Office, New Delhi.

The Copyright Board consists of Chairman and a minimum of two and maximum of fourteen members. However, according to Section 11 of The Copyright (Amendment) Act, 2012, the Copyright Board would have one Chairman and two members only. The Chairman of the copyright board is a person who is or has been a Judge of a High Court or is qualified for appointment as a Judge of High Court. The Registrar of copyrights acts as the Secretary of copyright board.

4.4 COPYRIGHT REGISTRATION IN INDIA

Copyright comes into existence, by default, the moment a document is created. However, one can get certificate of registration of copyright formally from the Copyright Office, i.e. at Copyright Division, Department of Higher Education, Ministry of Human Resource Development, New Delhi. There is also provision for online filing of copyright registration. The fee for registration of copyright varies from Fifty rupees (₹50) to Six Hundred rupees (₹600) depending on the type of document applied for copyright registration. The fee is to be paid in the name of Registrar of Copyrights, New Delhi.

The process of the copyright registration in India involves a series of steps (Figure 4.2). The applicant submits copyright registration application

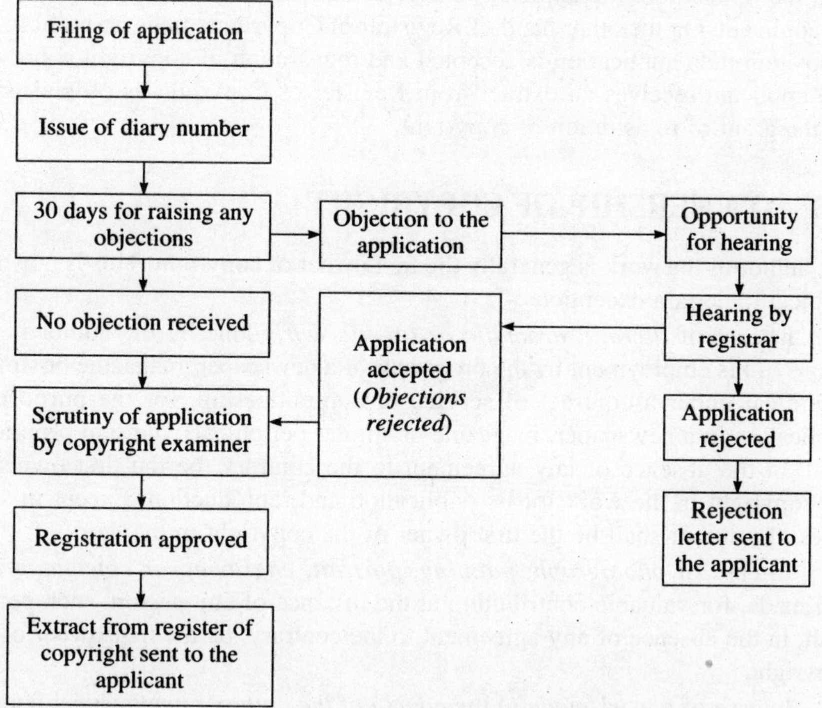

Figure 4.2 Process for Registration of Copyright.

along with the requisite fee, in the form of demand draft to the Copyright Office at New Delhi. The Statement of Purpose (SOP) and Statement of Further Particulars (SOFP) within the application (called as Form IV) should be compulsory signed by the applicant or by the lawyer in whose favour the Power of Attorney is given. Three copies of document for which the copyright is being applied are also submitted along with the application. A Diary Number is issued by the Copyright office after the submission of the application. Thirty days are given to the public to raise any objection regarding the document submitted for copyright registration. In case no objection is received within 30 days, the application along with said document whose copyright registration is being sought is scrutinized by the Copyright Examiner. In case of any discrepancy in the application or queries related to the document are there, these are sent to the applicant by post. If the answer sent by him/her is satisfactory, it is approved for registration of copyright. The applicant is sent an extract from Register of Copyright showing his approval of the copyright. The extract from the Register of Copyright is a legal document which may be produced in a court of law, in case of any copyright violation of the said document.

If any objection is received within 30 days, a letter is sent to both the parties and reply is sought within a specified time. Registrar of Copyrights listens to the reply from both the parties. If Registrar of Copyrights is satisfied with the opposition, the application is rejected and a rejection letter is sent to the applicant. On the other hand, if Registrar of Copyrights finds no merit in the opposition then application is accepted and registration of copyright approved. The applicant receives an extract from Register of Copyright as official proof for the grant of registration of copyright.

4.5 OWNERSHIP OF COPYRIGHT

The author of the work is generally the first owner of copyright. This is however "subject to certain exceptions:

In case of *literary, dramatic or artistic work* done by the author in the course of his employment by the proprietor of a newspaper, magazine or similar periodical under a contract of service or apprenticeship, for the purpose of publication in a newspaper, magazine or similar periodicals, the said proprietor shall, in the absence of any agreement to the contrary, be the first owner of the copyright in the work for its publication and reproduction. Except in such cases, the author shall be the first owner of the copyright in the work.

In case of *photograph, painting, portrait, engraving or cinematograph film* made, for valuable contribution at the instance of any person, such person shall, in the absence of any agreement to the contrary, be the first owner of the copyright.

In case of a *work made in the course of the author's employment* under a contract of service or apprenticeship, the employer shall, in the absence of any agreement to the contrary, be the first owner of copyright.

In case of *public speech*, the person who delivers the speech is the first owner of copyright. However, if the speech is delivered by someone on the behalf of another person, another person is first owner of the copyright.

In case of the Government work, the Government shall, the absence of any agreement to the contrary, be the first owner of the copyright".[2]

2. http://copyright.gov.in

4.5.1 Assignment of Copyright

Section 18 and 19 of the Copyright Act, 1957 states that the owner of the copyright in an existing work or the prospective owner of the copyright in a future work, may assign to any person the copyright either wholly or partially. In case of assignment of copyright in any future work, the assignment shall take effect only when the work comes into existence. For example, Novelists sell their copyright to publishers before the novel is complete. The assignor of the copyright will sign a written agreement specifying the specific rights assigned, duration and territorial extent of such assignment.

4.5.2 Licence of Copyright

Copyright is a bundle of rights having multiple benefits. The author of the work may licence the work to be printed in a book form, made into a film or converted into a drama format. In licence of the copyright, the ownership remains with the author. S/he may exploit the rights of the copyright as per her/his prerogative. In assignment, the ownership of the rights is transferred to the assignee. Section 30 and 31 of the Copyright Act, 1957 states that the owner of the copyright in any existing work or the prospective owner of the copyright in any future work may grant any interest in the right by licence in writing signed by him or by his duly authorized agent.

4.6 THE RIGHTS OF THE OWNER

Section 14 of the Copyright Act, 1957 provides the following "exclusive rights to the owner of copyright:

4.6.1 Literary, Dramatic or Musical Work (Not a Computer Program)

(i) To reproduce the work in any material form including the storing of it in any medium by electronics means

(ii) To issue copies of the work to the public not being copies already in circulation

(iii) To perform the work in public or communicate it to the public

(iv) To make cinematograph film or sound recording

(v) To make any translation of the work

(vi) To make any adaptation of the work

(vii) To do, in relation to a translation or an adaptation of the work, any of the acts specified in relation to the work given from (i) to (vi)

4.6.2 Computer Program

(i) All rights as specified to literary works (given above)
(ii) To sell or give on commercial rental or offer for sale or for commercial rental any copy of the computer program

4.6.3 Artistic Work

(i) To reproduce work in any material form including depiction in three dimensions of a two-dimensional work or in two dimensions of a three-dimensional work
(ii) To communicate the work to the public
(iii) To issue copies of work not in circulation
(iv) To include the work in any cinematograph film
(v) To make any adaptation of the work
(vi) To do in relation to an adaptation of the work any of the acts specified in relation to the work given from (i) to (vi)

4.6.4 Cinematograph Film

(i) To make a copy of the film including a photograph of any image forming part thereof
(ii) To sell or give on hire, or offer for sale or hire, any copy of the film
(iii) To communicate the film to the public

4.6.5 Sound Recording

(i) To make any other sound recording embodying it
(ii) To sell or give on hire, or offer for sale or hire, any copy of the sound recording
(iii) To communicate the sound recording to the public"[3]

The copyright also confers negative right to owner of the copyright, i.e. the owner of the copyright has to assert his right through a court of law in case of violation. It stops others from using its work without his/her permission.

4.7 TERM OF COPYRIGHT

The term of the copyright is generally lifetime of the author plus sixty years after his/her death, with some exceptions. The sixty year period is counted from beginning of the calendar year next following the year in which the author

3. http://copyright.gov.in

dies. In case of joint authorship, the sixty year period would be counted with reference to death of the author who dies last.

Some of the exceptions to the term of copyright are:

4.7.1 Anonymous and Pseudonymous Works

The term of copyright is only sixty years in case of a literary, dramatic, musical or artistic work, which is published anonymously or pseudonymously.

4.7.2 Posthumous Works

The term of copyright in posthumous work is sixty years.

4.7.3 Photographs

As per The Copyright (Amendment) Act, 2012, the term of copyright for photographs is lifetime of the author plus sixty years after his/her death.

4.7.4 Cinematograph Films

The term of copyright for cinematograph film is sixty years.

4.7.5 Sound Recording

The term of copyright for sound recording is sixty years.

4.7.6 Government Works

In cases where Government is the first owner of copyright, the term of the copyright is sixty years.

4.7.7 Public Undertaking

In cases where public undertaking is the first owner of copyright, the term of the copyright is sixty years.

4.7.8 International Organizations

In cases where international organization is the first owner of copyright, the term of the copyright is sixty years. The term begins from beginning of the calendar year next following the year in which the work is first published.

4.8 REGISTRATION OF COPYRIGHT

The Copyright Act provides for register of copyrights in which names or titles of work and the names and addresses of authors, publishers and owners of copyright and such other particulars as may be prescribed.

Section 45 of the Copyright Act, 1957 and Chapter VI of Copyright Rules, 1958 mentions the procedure for registration of copyright. The applicant will file the copyright application in triplicate, along with the prescribed fee, to the Copyright office at New Delhi. The applicant will also send notice to all interested parties about this application submission for getting copyright of the work, including the other authors in case of joint authorship. The Registrar of Copyright will enter the particulars of the work and details about the author of the work in the register of copyright, in case no objection is received within thirty days of the receipt of the application. In case, there is an objection, the Registrar will hear the parties, and decide the ownership of the copyright issue and accordingly enter details into the register of copyright. The Registrar will also send the copies of the entry to the owner of copyright. However, the registration of the work is not mandatory to claim protection under the Copyright Act.

4.9 BERNE CONVENTION AND UCC

The International Union for the Protection of Literary and Artistic work was established on 9 September 1886 in Berne (capital of Switzerland). It became effective since 5 December 1887. It has been revised five times, last being on 24 July 1971 at Paris. There were 137 countries as initial signatories to the 1971 text of the Convention. Under Berne Convention, copyright granted in a member country is valid across all member nation countries. However, the countries like USA, then USSR and China were not a part of Berne Convention. In order to facilitate these countries into adoption of international agreements, after due deliberations the Universal Copyright Convention (UCC) came into being on 10 July 1974. UCC as compared to Berne Convention had wider acceptability among the nations and copyright in one country was valid in all member countries. The main advantage of Berne Convention and UCC is that author of the work gets copyright in almost 150 member countries at one go. The authors, like in other IPRs, do not have to go from one country to the other for filing copyright.

4.10 RIGHTS OF BROADCASTING ORGANIZATION AND OF PERFORMERS

The broadcasting organizations, like Television and Radio have term of copyright for twenty-five years. Such rights are provided under 'Broadcast reproduction right' under Section 37 of the Copyright Act. As per the Act, "during the continuance of a broadcast reproduction right in relation to any broadcast, any person who, without licence of the owner of the right does the following acts of broadcast, would amount to infringement:

(a) Re-broadcasts the broadcast; or
(b) Causes the broadcast to be heard or seen by the public on payment of any charges; or
(c) Makes any sound recording or visual recording of the broadcast; or
(d) Makes any reproduction of such sound recording or visual recording where such initial recording was done without licence or, where it was licensed, for any purpose not envisaged by such licence; or
(e) Sells or hires to the public, or offers for such sale or hire, any such sound recording or visual recording referred to in (c) or (d).

The performer's rights for term of copyright subsist until fifty years. During the continuance of a performer's right in relation to any performance, any person who, without the consent of the performer, does any of the following acts, would amount to infringement:

(a) Makes a sound recording or visual recording of the performance; or
(b) Reproduces a sound recording or visual recording of the performance; or
(c) Broadcasts the performance; or
(d) Communicates the performance to the public otherwise than by broadcast".[4]

However, once a performer gives his consent for his act in a cinematograph film, the performer loses the right to complain about the above-mentioned infringement.

The copyright being a negative right, the owner has to assert his right of copyright in case of violation. The broadcaster's right and performer's right of the copyright are created the moment it is broadcast or performed. The infringement clauses point towards the rights, an owner of the copyright holds and may sue for infringement in case he feels that his rights of copyright have been violated.

4.11 INTERNATIONAL COPYRIGHT

India is signatory of Berne Convention and Universal Copyright Convention (UCC), and hence, copyright assigned in India are valid across all member nations of Berne Convention and UCC. Similarly, copyright assigned in any of these member countries is valid in India and provided protection under Indian Copyright Act. The term of copyright of a foreign work will be equivalent to

4. http://parliamentofindia.nic.in/ls/bills/1994/1994-31.htm

the term of copyright in the country of origin and not the term as per Indian Copyright Act.

4.12 INFRINGEMENT OF COPYRIGHT

The rights of the copyright are protected against any kind of infringement to promote and motivate the author for creating and inventing new works. These works may be published, stored, reproduced, translated or adapted in different forms by the author. The author may also exploit it for monetary benefits by way of licensing or assignment. As per Section 51 of the Copyright Act, 1957 and subsequent amendments the copyright in a work shall be "deemed to be infringed when:

(a) Any person without a valid licence
  - Does anything, the exclusive right to do so is with the owner of the copyright
  - Permits for profit any place to be used for the communication of the work to the public where such communication constitutes an infringement of the copyright in the work

(b) Any person
  - Makes for sale or hire, or sells or lets for hire, or by way of trade displays or offers for sale or hire, or
  - Distributes either for the purpose of trade or to such an extent as to effect prejudicially the owner of the copyright, or
  - By way of trade exhibits in public, or
  - Imports into India"[5]

any infringing copies of the work.

However, before looking into the infringement of the copyright, one should check the term of the copyright. For example, a single author wrote a book on Calculus in the year 1927. The author died in 1941. Some parts of a chapter of Calculus book were taken by another author verbatim as a part of a chapter of his new book in 2005, with due acknowledgement. This is not infringement of copyright as the term of copyright has expired after sixty years after the death of the author. Also downloading certain copyright material from the internet for judicial proceedings, educational purpose or its non-commercial use is also not an infringement of copyright.

4.13 REMEDIES AGAINST COPYRIGHT INFRINGEMENT

The Indian Copyright Act provides civil and criminal remedies against infringement of copyright. Section 55 of the Act provides civil remedies which

5. http://copyright.gov.in

includes injunction, damages, account of profit and confiscation of infringement material. For example, a movie is made exactly on a novel without the consent of the author, who holds the copyright of the novel. The plaintiff, i.e. the author of the novel, on approaching court for the copyright violation, may be granted injunction, i.e. stopping the further screening of the movie with immediate effect or stopping the release of the movie in case it is not yet released. The court may grant certain amount of damages as it deems fit for the copyright infringement. An account of profit relief means giving back the profit amount that the producer of the movie may have earned by infringing the copyright of the plaintiff. The court may order confiscation of all the infringed copy of the movie so as it is not further used or reproduced. Section 58 of the Act states that "all infringing copies of any work in which copyright subsists, and all plates used or intended to be used for the production of such infringing copies, shall be deemed to be the property of the owner of the copyright".

Section 63 of the Act provides for criminal remedies against copyright infringement. It states that "an offence of infringement of copyright shall be punishable with imprisonment for a term which shall not be less than six months, but which may extend to three years and with fine which of fifty thousand rupees to two lakh rupees". Section 63A provides "a stringent penalty for second and subsequent offence of infringement. In such cases the imprisonment term shall not be less than one year but which may extend to three years and with fine which shall not be less than one lakh rupees but which may extend to two lakhs rupees". Further, if any person knowingly makes use on a computer of an infringing copy of a computer program shall be punishable with imprisonment for a term which shall not be less than seven days, but which may extend to three years and with fine of fifty thousand rupees to two lakhs rupees.

4.14 THE COPYRIGHT (AMENDMENT) ACT, 2012

The Copyright (Amendment) Act, 2012 came into effect from 21 June 2012. These amendments have made The Copyright Act more in line with WIPO treaties besides incorporating issues related to digital storage and digital transmission of copyrighted material. It also made changes in Performers rights so as provide royalty to performers like singers and composers each time it is broadcast or commercialized.

Section 14 has been amended for providing "electronic storage" apart from other mediums as part of reproduction of copyrighted material. It also allows for "depiction in three dimensions of a two-dimensional work" and vice-versa. Section 22 provided copyright for photograph for a period of 60 years after the death of copyright holder which was earlier 60 years only. Section 31 of the Copyright Act, 1957 which dealt with compulsory licensing was amended to make broader in ambit by replacing the word "any Indian work" with "any work". Section 31-A of the Amendment allows compulsory licences where "any work is withheld from the public in India and author is dead or unknown or cannot be traced". Also, Section 31-B allows for compulsory licence to anyone working for benefit of the disabled. The Copyright Board responds to such application within two months. Section 33 provides for changes in registration of copyright society. All the existing copyright societies had to do fresh registration within one year. The new registration would be valid for 5 years, and it may be renewed again. Section 35 states that "Every copyright society would have governing body with an equal number of authors and owners of work".

Section 38 of The Copyright (Amendment) Act, 2012 provides due rights to performer of a performance in terms of his "right to claim to be identified as the performer of his performance" and "to restrain or claim damages in respect of any distortion, mutilation or other modification of his performance that would be prejudicial to his reputation". Section 52 provides provisions of fair use, i.e. specific acts which are not considered a copyright violation. It includes any incidental storage of item in electronic form; preparation of any work in Braille; reproduction of any work for judicial proceedings and reproduced material prepared by Secretariat of Legislature for exclusive usage by members of the Legislature.

4.15 THE INFORMATION TECHNOLOGY ACT, 2000

This Act facilitates rising e-commerce business in India besides providing legal validity and security to business transaction using digital signatures. The Act which originally came into being on 17 October 2000 has gone through changes in 2003, 2004, 2008, 2009, 2011 and 2013. The IT Act, 2000 is divided into thirteen chapters. Chapter I provides precise definition of important IT related terms which are frequently used in business transactions. For example, Section 2(t) mentions "electronic record" means "data, record or data generated, image or sound stored, received or sent in an electronic form or micro film or computer generated micro fiche". Chapter II and III gives detail about legal considerations in authentication of digital signature and electronic signatures besides rules for facilitating electronic governance. The provisions of IT Act, 2000 and IT (Amendment) Act, 2008 provides validity to different forms of electronic signatures. Given the diversity of Indian populations in terms of literacy, awareness and access to technology, providing different options for authentication would go a long way to facilitate business operations and provide seamless government services to the public. The IT (Amendment) Act, 2008 came into effect from 27 October 2009.

Chapter IV to VII consist of laws regarding handing of electronic records including its security, dispatch and about certifying authorities. It specifies the onus of data security in case of its breach. This would provide confidence and protection to the businesses which have high frequency and quantum of data transfer including the business process outsourcing companies. The Chapter VI of the Act lays down terms for appointment and functions of

Controller of Certifying Authorities. The Controller lays down "the standards to be maintained by the Certifying authorities" and ensures their proper conduct. The Certifying Authorities would issue Digital Signature Certificates (DSC) and maintain a repository of the same. The provisions for grant, suspension and rejection of licenses for issuing DSCs are enumerated in detail in Chapter VII of The IT Act, 2000.

Chapter VIII lay down duties of electronic signature subscribers besides rules for generation and control of private key. The penalty and compensation provisions are covered under Chapter IX of The IT Act, 2000. It also provides details about the adjudication process including the key factors to be taken into consideration while hearing the parties regarding violation of electronic signature related issues. Chapter X enumerates rules regarding establishment, composition and powers of Cyber Appellate Tribunal. The various kind of offences related to electronic signature and computer related offences and their penalty is covered in Chapter XI. Exemption of certain intermediaries from any kind of liability is covered in Chapter XII. The last chapter, i.e. Chapter XIII covers miscellaneous issues like power of police officers in IT related cases, protection from any IT act done in good faith and power of Controller or Central Government to make new rules.

4.16 INTERNET AND COPYRIGHT ISSUES

The increasing penetration of IT (Information Technology) and internet in India is making internet usage more common across the country. Individuals and organizations have access to plethora of information on the internet. At times, they themselves also upload information and knowledge content over the internet. Since creation of any content requires resources and is copyrighted, using any piece of these resources without acknowledging the source may amount to copyright infringement. The general perception is that if there is copyright warning or the copyright symbol is mentioned, then only it is copyright protected. However, it is not so, any content created by the rightful owner on the internet is copyright protected, irrespective of the copyright warning. No doubt, the warning acts as deterrence against any possible violation. The Government of India has made two major laws, viz. Copyright Act, 1957 and Information Technology Act, 2000 to ensure copyright protection and also to facilitate secure electronic communication and commerce in the country. One of the famous cases in copyright violation on internet is Himalaya Drug Company versus Sumit. Himalaya Drug Company claimed that its herbal database displayed on the company website was verbatim copied and reproduced by website run by Sumit. The herbal products website of Sumit came in being two year after Himalaya Drug Company uploaded this herbal database. The court through various evidences found the copyright infringement claims of Himalaya Drug Company to be true. The Delhi High Court in its final ruling besides ordering permanent injunction also ordered rupees 7.94 lakhs as compensatory damages against Sumit to be paid to Himalaya Drug Company.

4.17 SUMMARY

The copyright in India is governed by The Copyright Act, 1957. The Act has been amended many times, the latest major amendment being in 1999, in order to bring it in conformity with the international conventions like TRIPs, Berne Convention and Universal Copyright Convention (UCC). Copyright provides protection to literary works which includes computer programmes, tables and compilations; dramatic works; musical works; artistic works; cinematograph films; and sound recordings. The unique thing about copyright is that copyright comes into existence by default the moment a work is created. However, one can get certificate of registration of copyright formally also from the Copyright Office. Unlike patent which is a territorial right, copyright work created in India gets total copyright related protection and privileges in all Berne Convention and UCC signatory countries. The copyright may be transferred to third party by way of assignment of copyright or by licence of copyright. The term of the copyright is lifetime of the author plus sixty years after his/her death, with some exceptions. The sixty-year period is counted from the beginning of the calendar year next following the year in which the author dies. In case of joint authorship, the sixty year period would be counted with reference to the death of the author who dies last. The broadcasting organizations, like Television and Radio have term of copyright for twenty-five years. Such rights are provided under 'Broadcast reproduction right' under Section 37 of the Copyright Act. The Copyright Act provides for register of copyrights in which names or titles of work and the names and addresses of authors, publishers and owners of copyright are recorded. It is one of most important legal document referred to in cases of ownership related copyright disputes. The rights of the copyright are protected against any kind of infringement to promote and motivate the author for creating and inventing new works. The Indian Copyright Act provides civil and criminal remedies against infringement of copyright. Section 55 of the Act provides civil remedies which includes injunction, damages, account of profit and confiscation of infringement material. With the pervasiveness usage of information technology in almost every process, the issues related to copyright infringement and protection has become quite challenging now.

CASE STUDY—GOOGLE LIBRARY PROJECT

In December 2004, Google announced its Google Book Search Library Project. The ambitious project aimed at digitizing all library books and making it available online at Google platform. This announcement was met with lot of enthusiasm worldwide and also with critical opposition citing copyright infringement issues. Since then, Google had already scanned millions of books across different libraries in USA and other countries. The target was to scan and make available around 30 million books online to its viewers. There are three types of books—one, whose term of copyright has expired; two, whose term of copyright is still remaining, but is out of print; and three, the term of copyright is remaining and also it is also in print. For Google there was no problem in accessing the first type as the copyright has expired and it can be accessed by everyone. Google implemented Google Partner programme for the third category of books. The publisher whomsoever owns the copyright is free to join Google Partner programme. The google viewers would get limited access to such type of book. This will help in promotion and increasing sales of the book. However, in cases of second category of books, i.e. where the term of copyright is still remaining but the books are out of print; Google can access those books only through libraries. Many of the libraries have signed agreement allowing Google to scan these books. Among these scanned books for Google Library Project were also those books for which their publishers had not joined the Google Partner programme. Authors Guild which has around 8000 authors as its member filed a complaint against Google in September, 2004 claiming that the Google Library Project was a major violation of copyright. This was followed by several similar suits of copyright violation in USA by publisher associations against Google Library Project. There were suits filed by Germany and France publishers against Google in their respective countries alleging copyright violation by Google Library Project. Google argued that it is fair use and it was only letting access a part of the copyright material through snippets and not the entire book. It will help promote the books and make the information universally accessible. However, petitioners argued that Google has no right under copyright rules to keep the complete book in digitized form in its Google Library Project repository.

ISSUES FOR DISCUSSION

1. How is digitizing the first category of books under Google Library Project not a copyright violation? Explain with an example.
2. Microsoft started a similar project called Live Search Books in 2006, but abandoned the project after two years. What future do you see for Google Library Project in such a scenario?
3. Discuss the copyright issues involved in Google Library Project.

Discussion Questions

1. "The author of the work is generally the first owner of copyright. This is however subject to certain exceptions". Elaborate these exceptions where the author of the work is not the first owner of copyright.
2. Enumerate the classes of work which The Copyright Act, 1957 covers for protection of copyright.
3. What are works covered under literary class as per The Copyright Act, 1957?
4. Discuss the series of steps involved in process of the copyright registration in India.

5. What are the rights of the owner of copyright?
6. What is the term of copyright in case of posthumous works and cinematograph films?
7. What are Berne Convention and UCC?
8. Explain what amounts to infringement of copyright as per The Copyright Act, 1957.
9. Elaborate the copyright privileges of broadcasting organization and of performers in India.
10. What are the remedies provided under The Copyright Act, 1957 against copyright infringement?

Objective Type Questions

Tick the right answer in given multiple-choice questions:

1. Literary works include
   (a) Computer programs (b) Tables (c) Computer databases
   (d) All of them
2. The term of copyright for government works is
   (a) 40 years (b) 50 years (c) 60 years (d) 70 years
3. The Berne Convention became effective since
   (a) 5 December 1887 (b) 5 December 1997
   (c) 5 December 2000 (d) 5 December 2009
4. UCC stands for
   (a) Universal Copyright Convention (b) United Copyright Convention
   (c) United Copyright Centre (d) Universal Copyright Centre
5. The number of days given for public to raise any objection regarding the document submitted for copyright registration are:
   (a) 18 days (b) 20 days (c) 21 days (d) 30 days
6. Which of the following is not a subject matter of copyright
   (a) Musical Works (b) An Idea (c) Artistic Works (d) Sound Recording
7. The copyright office is located at
   (a) Chennai (b) Mumbai (c) New Delhi (d) Kolkata
8. The term of copyright for sound recordings is
   (a) 30 years (b) 40 years (c) 50 years (d) 60 years
9. The infringement of copyright attract
   (a) Civil Suit (b) Criminal Suit (c) None of them (d) Both of them
10. The Registrar of copyright acts as .... of copyright board.
   (a) Chairman (b) Secretary (c) Treasurer (d) None of them

Mark TRUE or FALSE against given statements:

1. The author of the work is always the first owner of copyright. (True / False)
2. A Diary Number is issued by the Copyright office after the submission of the copyright registration application. (True / False)
3. The copyright comes into existence by default the moment a work is created. (True / False)
4. The Indian Copyright Act provides only civil remedies against infringement of copyright. (True / False)
5. Copyright work created in India gets total copyright related protection and privileges in all Berne Convention and UCC signatory countries. (True / False)

References

Ashok, Arathi (2010), "Economic Rights of Authors under Copyright Law: Some Emerging Judicial Trends", *Journal of Intellectual Property Rights*, Volume 15, pp. 35–45.

Chindalia, Sanjanaa (2008), "Open Source Software: The Future Ahead", *Journal of Intellectual Property Rights*, Volume 13, pp. 218–224.

Ghosh, Rishab Aiyer (2007), "IPR, Law and FLOSS: Building a Protected Common", *Journal of Intellectual Property Rights*, Volume 12, pp. 176–182.

Nayak, Abhipsa and Chatterjee, Satabdi (2010), "Onset of mobile chip piracy in the domain of Copyright Infringement", *Journal of Intellectual Property Rights*, Volume 15, pp. 117–121.

Pandey, Geetika, and Pandey, Neeraj (2006), "Copyrights Issues in Software: An Indian Perspective", Proceedings of the National Seminar on Copyrights: Emerging Issues in India; pp. 42–45.

Pandey, Neeraj and Bhattacharya, K.K.(2008), "The Academia Dynamics in New Intellectual Property Regime in Third World Countries", *Journal of the World Universities Forum*, Volume 1, Number 2, pp. 1–7.

Some Questions and Answers on Patents, Copyrights, Designs, Trademarks, IC Layout Designs, Geographical Indications, Patent Facilitating Centre, TIFAC, New Delhi, 2005.

The Copyright Act, 1957 Bare Acts, Universal Law Publishing, 2010.

The Copyright Act, 1957 Bare Acts, Professional Book Publishers, 2014.

The Information Technology Act, 2000 Bare Acts, Professional Book Publishers, 2014.

Websites

http://copyright.gov.in

http://people.ischool.berkeley.edu/~hal/Papers/2006/google-library.pdf

http://www.wipo.int

CHAPTER 5

Trade Marks

Trade Marks are integral part of the business. IBM, Airtel, Coca Cola, Godrej, Tata, Levis, Dell, Nokia, Titan and Apple are trade marks which have got high brand equity and goodwill. Trade Marks are also used to convey quality and product differentiation. Customers are ready to pay a premium for established trade marks. Trade Marks are nurtured and built over the years, and so it need to be protected against any commercial misuse. The nomenclature and design of a trade mark should be judiciously done so that it is unique and connects with the product persona. This is important as there is a clutter of large number of trade marks in each category of business.

The Trade and Merchandise Marks Act, 1958 was the original act governing trade marks in India. It had been amended many times before 1999. However, due to opening up of economy in 1991, increased globalization of trade and business and to align trade mark laws with WTO requirements, a comprehensive review of The Trade and Merchandise Marks Act, 1958 was taken up in 1999 and many changes were incorporated. As a result new revised act called as The Trade Marks Act, 1999 came into being.

5.1 WHAT IS A TRADE MARK?

Section 1 of The Trade Marks Act, 1999 states that "Trade Mark means a mark capable of being represented graphically and which is capable of distinguishing the goods or services of one person from those of others and may include shape of goods, their packaging and combination of colours". The mark in Trade Mark includes a device, brand, heading, label/ ticket, name, signature, word, letter, numeral, shape of goods, packaging or combinations of colours or any combination of the above. The service in Trade Mark includes the provision of services in connection with business of any industrial or commercial matters, such as banking, communication, education, financing, insurance, chit funds, real estate, transport, entertainment, amusement, construction, repair, conveying of news or information and advertising.

The Trade Mark is basically used by businesses to identify their product or services and their origin. Xerox, McDonalds, KFC, Google, Microsoft, HCL, LG, etc. are unique trade marks, which help differentiate them and their products and services from others. Trade Mark also conveys certain level of product quality and service support expectation from the organization which owns it. The customers expect better product and services from established trade marks as they pay premium to acquire them.

5.2 DEVELOPING A TRADE MARK

The organization should invest sufficient time and money to develop and finalize a Trade Mark as it exists till the entire life of product or services. The unique Trade Mark will facilitate better promotion and sales of the brand. It would add value to the product or service and provide visibility. For example, Pizza Hut is a better trade mark as the nomenclature is appealing and reflects its core competence in pizza related products.

The nomenclature and colour scheme should ensure that it is new and fresh. This will help the trade mark to stand out of the clutter and deter its violation. At times, coining totally new words, that are not a part of any dictionary, also gives unique visibility. Strength of such Trade Mark is strong in the sense that no can easily misuse or infringe it. For example, Xerox and Exxon were completely new words and the Trade Marks became an instant hit.

Apart from being distinct in nomenclature and colour, a Trade Mark should be easy to pronounce. It should be a catchy word and preferably small. A single word like LG, Rin, Tide, Pepsi, GM, Panchranga, Indica, Nano, Estallio, etc. would be a better choice. It should be soothing to eyes and ears and should reflect quality.

5.3 CONDITIONS FOR TRADE MARK REGISTRATION

Section 9 of The Trade Marks Act, 1999 provides certain exception for which Trade Mark cannot be granted in India. These absolute grounds for "refusal of registration of trade marks is further categorized into three conditions:

5.3.1 Absolute Ground of Refusal (Section 9)

First Condition for Absolute Ground for Refusal of Registration of Trade Marks

1. A mark which are devoid of any distinctive character
2. A mark which consist exclusively of marks or indications which may serve in trade to designate the kind, quality, quantity, intended purpose, values, geographical origin or the time of production of the

goods or rendering of the service or other characteristics of the goods or service

3. A mark which consist exclusively of marks or indications which have become customary in the current language or in the *bona fide* and established practices of trade

However, a Trade Mark shall not be refused registration if before the date of application for registration it has acquired a distinctive character as a result of the use made of it or a well-known trade mark.

Second Condition for Absolute Ground for Refusal of Registration of Trade Marks

1. A mark is of such nature as to deceive the public or cause confusion
2. A mark which contains or comprises any matter likely to hurt the religious susceptibilities of any class or section of the citizens of India
3. A mark which comprises or contains scandalous or obscene matter
4. A mark whose use is prohibited under the Emblems and Names (Prevention of Improper Use) Act, 1950

Third Condition for Absolute Ground for Refusal of Registration of Trade Marks

1. A mark consists exclusively of the shape of goods which results from the nature of the goods themselves
2. A mark consists exclusively of the shape of goods which is necessary to obtain a technical result
3. A mark consists exclusively of the shape which gives substantial value to the goods"[1]

5.3.2 Relative Ground of Refusal (Section 11)

1. A mark whose identity with an earlier Trade Mark and similarity of goods or services covered by the trade mark, for example, a Trade Mark will not be granted if a company 'A' in footwear industry is asking for a 'Bata' Trade Mark. The reason is that the Trade Mark is already in use and the applicant is also in same category of product or services as 'Bata'. This will cause confusion on the part of the public who may draw association with the earlier Trade Mark.
2. A mark which is identical or similar to an earlier Trade Mark; and is to be registered for goods or services which are not similar to those for which the earlier Trade Mark is registered in the name of

1. http://www.wipo.int

a different proprietor. In such cases, a mark will not be registered, if or to the extent, the earlier trade mark is a well-known Trade Mark in India and the use of the later mark without due cause would take unfair advantage of or be detrimental to the distinctive character or repute of the earlier Trade Mark.

A 'well-known trade mark' as per The Trade Marks Act, 1999 means a mark which has become so to the substantial segment of the public which uses such goods or receives such services that the use of such mark in relation to other goods or services would be likely to be taken as indicating a connection in the course of trade or rendering of services between those goods or services and a person using the mark in relation to the first-mentioned goods or services.

This means that a mark may become trade marked if the one already in use is not a well-known Trade Mark. For example, a company in foods and beverages want to use 'Intel' brand stating that it is operating in different industry segment, and hence, the Trade Mark be granted. In such cases a Trade Mark is never granted as per The Trade Marks Act, 1999. The reason is that 'Intel' is a well-known Trade Mark, and due to this customers might associate some linkages between 'Intel' and the foods & beverages company. This might in turn affect 'Intel' Trade Mark's goodwill and brand equity. However, the same foods and beverages company applies for a trade mark for goods or services which are not similar to those for which the earlier trade mark is registered in the name of a different proprietor; and the Trade Mark is not well-known, then the foods and beverages company may get the same Trade Mark subject to discretion of Registrar of Trade Marks.

5.4 REGISTER OF TRADE MARKS

Section 6 of The Trade Marks Act, 1999 provides for a Register of Trade Marks. It is kept at the head office of the Trade Marks Registry. It keeps a record of all registered trade marks with the names, addresses and description of the proprietors; notifications of assignment and transmissions; the names, addresses and descriptions of registered users; conditions; limitations and all other matter relating to registered Trade Marks. It is a legal document. It is one of most important document referred to in case of Trade Mark disputes between two or more parties.

5.5 TRENDS IN TRADE MARKS APPLICATIONS

There has been consistent increase in the number of Trade Mark applications over the years. About 1.84 lakhs (0.184 million) Trade Mark applications were filed in 2011–2012 (Table 5.1). Usually domestic applicants are more than the foreign applicants in case of Trade Mark applications (Table 5.2). The different type of Trade Mark filed for registration includes word marks; device marks; number marks; letter marks and letter and numeral marks (Table 5.3).

Table 5.1 Trade Mark Applications in India

Year	*2005–06*	*2006–07*	*2007–08*	*2008–09*	*2009–10*	*2010–11*	*2011–12*
Filed	85699	103419	123514	130172	141943	179317	183588
Examined	77500	85185	63605	105219	25875	205065	116263
Registered	184325	109361	100857	102257	67490	115472	51735

Source: Annual Report, Office of Controller General of Patents, Designs, Trade Marks & Geographical Indications, India 2009–2010; 2010–2011 and 2011–2012.

Table 5.2 Trends in Trade Mark Applications

Year	*2005–06*	*2006–07*	*2007–08*	*2008–09*	*2009–10*	*2010–11*	*2011–12*
Indian	73308	88210	117014	119371	134403	167701	169602
Foreign	12361	15209	6500	10801	7540	11616	13986
Total	85669	103419	123514	130172	141943	179317	183588

Source: Annual Report, Office of Controller General of Patents, Designs, Trade Marks & Geographical Indications, India 2009–2010; 2010–2011 and 2011–2012.

Table 5.3 Different Types of Trade Marks

Types of Marks	*2008–2009*	*2009–2010*	*2010–2011*	*2011–2012*
Word Marks	51082	68835	77454	62205
Device Marks	79059	73039	101851	121006
Number Marks	–	26	5	358
Letter Marks	31	1	7	19
Letter and Numeral	–	42	–	–
Total	130172	141943	179317	183588

Source: Annual Report, Office of Controller General of Patents, Designs, Trade Marks & Geographical Indications, India 2009–2010; 2010–2011 and 2011–2012.

According to the annual report released by Office of CGPDTM (Controller General of Patents, Designs and Trade Marks) for 2011–2012, there are more than one lakh Trade Mark applications pending before the Trade Mark Registry. The main reason behind this backlog is shortage of adequate manpower in Trade Mark Registry. CGPDTM had taken series of steps to reduce this trade mark applications backlog. The Trade Mark Registry is now following 'first come first serve' rule in disposing off the cases. This has enabled Trade mark Registry to focus on the backlog cases stuck at various stages of inspection. The Trade Mark activities were decentralized to local Trade Mark branch offices for convenience of the public. These initiatives along with introduction of electronic filling and registration of applications, has also brought transparency and better effectiveness in Trade Mark services.

5.6 PROCEDURE FOR TRADE MARK REGISTRATION IN INDIA

There is a step wise procedure for grant of Trade Mark (Figure 5.1). Section 18 of The Trade Marks Act, 1999 provides for the procedure of Trade Mark registration in India. Firstly, the applicant claiming to be the proprietor of a Trade Mark used or proposed to be used by him/her and desirous of registering it, shall submit an application in the prescribed format to the Registrar of Trade Marks. A single application is made for registration of a Trade Mark for different classes of goods and services. However, the fees should be paid in respect of each such class of goods or services. The application has to be filed only in the office of the Trade Marks Registry according to location of the business.

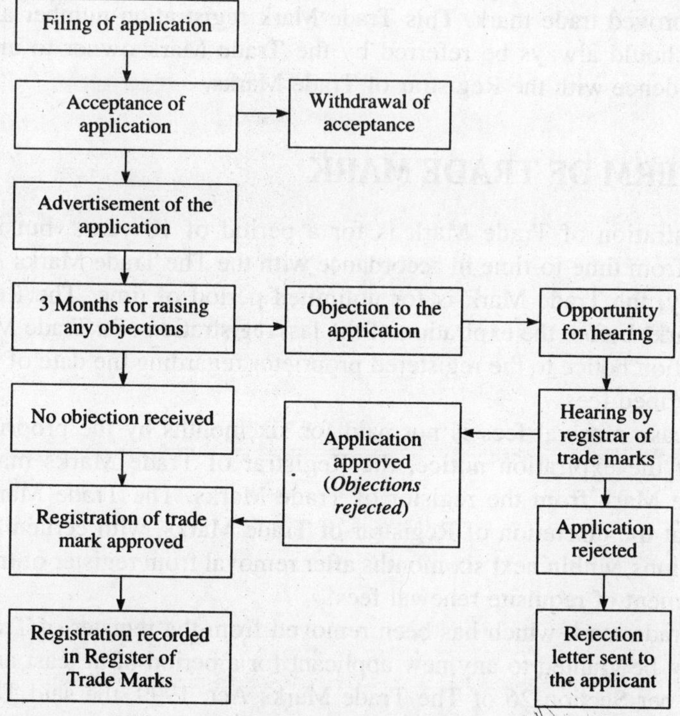

Figure 5.1 Process for Registration of Trade Mark.

The Head office of Trade Marks Registry is in Mumbai, with its branch offices at Kolkata, New Delhi, Chennai and Ahmedabad.

The Registrar of Trade Marks may accept or reject the application. The Registrar may also ask for some amendments and after those amendments may accept the application. Even after the acceptance of the application, Registrar may withdraw the acceptance of application within two months if it is found that the application had been accepted in error. The applicant is informed of the withdrawal of the acceptance and depending upon his reply/amendments and subsequent hearing by the Registrar, the application is finally accepted or not accepted.

After the acceptance of application for Trade Mark registration, the Registrar will issue an advertisement. Three months are given to the public to raise any objection regarding the Trade Mark due for the registration. In case no objection is received within 3 months, the registration of Trade Mark is approved. In case any opposition is received, these are sent to the applicant by post, and it has to be replied by the applicant within 2 months of receipt of the notice. After Registrar receives the reply from the applicant, there is hearing of both or all the parties. The Registrar approves the registration of Trade Mark if the opposition for registration is rejected and vice-versa. The registration is recorded in the Register of Trade Marks, along with name of the proprietor. A unique Trade Mark registration number with the current date is allocated to the approved trade mark. This Trade Mark registration number along with the date should always be referred by the Trade Mark owner to any further correspondence with the Registrar of Trade Marks.

5.7 TERM OF TRADE MARK

The registration of Trade Mark is for a period of 10 years, but it may be renewed from time-to-time in accordance with the The Trade Marks Act, 1999. Practically, the Trade Mark is for unlimited period of time. The Registrar of Trade Marks before the expiration of the last registration of a Trade Mark sends an expiration notice to the registered proprietor regarding the date of expiration and prescribed fees.

In case renewal fees is not paid for six months by the proprietor, after expiry of the expiration notice, the Registrar of Trade Marks may remove the Trade Mark from the register of Trade Marks. The Trade Mark may be restored at the discretion of Registrar of Trade Marks, with certain conditions or limitations, within next six months after removal from register of trade marks after payment of requisite renewal fees.

A trade mark which has been removed from the register of Trade Marks would not be granted to any new applicant for a period of at least another one year. As per Section 26 of The Trade Marks Act, 1999, the said Trade Mark for the purpose of any application for the registration of another Trade Mark during one year, next after the date of removal, is deemed to be a Trade Mark already on the register.

5.8 ASSIGNMENT AND TRANSMISSION

The registered proprietor of Trade Mark, whose name appears in the register of Trade Marks, has the power to assign or transmit the Trade Mark for any consideration. As per The Trade Marks Act, 1999 assignment of Trade Marks means an assignment in writing by act of the parties concerned. Transmission means transmission by operation of law, devolution on the personal representative of a deceased person and any other mode of transfer, not being assignment.

Trade Mark may be assigned or transmitted by the registered proprietor, provided it does not give multiple exclusive rights to more than one of the person for the same good or service or same description of goods or services. However, it may be done in case goods or services are to be sold in different markets. The Registrar, if satisfied by the documentary proof, may allow registering the name of parties whom the assignment or transmission of Trade Mark had been done by registered proprietor.

5.9 MADRID SYSTEM

Trade Mark is a territorial right, i.e. the owner of the Trade Mark has to register Trade Mark separately in all countries wherever it intends to do trade in that product or services in future. This is important so that no one in other country registers the said Trade Mark in its own name. It requires a lot of time and money on the part of the owner of the Trade Mark to get it registered in many countries separately. However, with the coming into force of Madrid System, the owner of the Trade Mark may get Trade Mark protected in all the Madrid Agreement signatory countries through one application form with his own national Trade Mark office. An applicant to avail advantages of Madrid System must be a national of member country. The applicant should first register the mark in his own country. This is known as 'basic registration'. After the 'basic registration' it is forwarded for international registration under Madrid System. The protocol related to the Madrid Agreement was adopted in 1989 and it came into force in December, 1995. The Madrid System has facilitated better management of trade mark by companies or individual owners of Trade Marks.

5.10 COLLECTIVE MARKS

As per Section 61 of The Trade Marks Act, 1999; collective marks are Trade Marks distinguishing the goods or services of members of an association of persons which is the proprietor of the mark from those of others. A collective mark may not be granted if it is likely to deceive or cause confusion among the public. Collective marks are applied after members involved in selling similar goods or services form an association and apply for Trade Mark registration. The collective Trade Mark can be used by all the members of the association for marketing their goods or services. The association is the owner of Trade Mark and the members of the association are registered users of the Trade Mark. It helps in saving time and money, especially for small manufacturers and traders. The association also ensures that there is no misuse of Trade Mark by any non-member organization.

5.11 CERTIFICATION TRADE MARK

Certification Trade Mark is a special kind of mark which distinguishes the goods or services by certifying it regarding the origin, material, mode of manufacturing, quality, accuracy, etc. The certificate is issued by the proprietor of the mark. For example, ISI certification mark is issued by Bureau of Indian Standards (BIS). The ISI certification mark certifies that the product is quality tested. Similarly, like BIS any other agency which wants to issue quality or any other type of product or services certification may apply for certification Trade Mark. The process for issue of certification Trade Mark is similar to the process of issue of other Trade Marks.

5.12 INFRINGEMENT OF TRADE MARK

Section 29 of The Trade Marks Act, 1999 states that a registered Trade Mark is said to be infringed by a person who, not being a registered proprietor, uses in the course of trade, a mark which is identical with, or deceptively similar to, the Trade Mark in relation to good or services in respect of which the Trade Mark is registered and in such manner as to render the use of the mark likely to be taken as being used as a Trade Mark. Thus, there may be three major types of infringement:

1. The infringed Trade Mark is identical to registered proprietor's Trade Mark
2. The infringed Trade Mark contains complete or a part of registered proprietor's Trade Mark features combined with other matter
3. The infringed Trade Mark is deceptively similar to registered proprietor's Trade Mark. For example, in phonetics, like Lakme and Like-me or in brand spelling like Britannia and Bricannia

Overall if any person, who is not a registered proprietor, uses in course of trade a mark which is similar or identical with the registered Trade Mark due to which it is likely to cause confusion amongst the public or likely to show an association with the registered Trade Mark, it amounts to an infringement.

The onus of proving an infringement of a trade mark in a court of law lies with registered proprietor of trade mark. It has to be proved that there was unauthorized usage of trade mark by deception or otherwise by the third party for commercial gain. Also, in order to deter unauthorized usage of trade mark or similar deceptive marks, a public notice through Trade Mark attorney may be published in newspaper (Figure 5.2). For example, The Gujarat Tea Depot Company found that in some parts of India its Trade Mark "Good Morning" was used in unauthorized way for marketing different products. It issued a common legal notice against those organizations which were infringing the trade mark. This kind of legal notice in public apart from providing deterrence to unauthorized trade mark users, also strengthens the legal case from proprietor's perspective.

Trade Mark Caution Notice

Our Clients, **THE GUJARAT TEA DEPOT CO.**, of Krishna Estate, Nr. Pragati High School, Khokhra Mehemdabad, Ahmedabad-380008 are the common law and statutory owners of the trademark.

Trade Mark: "GOOD MORNING"

Which is registered in their name under numbers 91340 dated. 15th January, 1944 & 475596 dated: 21st July, 1987, in respect of tea, coffee, coffee substitutes, spices, flavours and flavouring for tea and coffee and sugar in class 30, under the Trade Marks Act.

By virtue of the above, our said clients enjoy rights to the exclusive use of this trademark in respect of their aforesaid products for sale all over India and also for export.

At present The Gujarat Tea Depot Co. has entered into an agreement with Gujarat Tea Processors and Packers Ltd. and has permitted the use of said Good Morning Trade Mark.

Notice is hereby given to all to whom it may concern that use of the aforesaid trademark or trademark(s) deceptively similar thereto, by any person(s) not authorised by our clients, in respect of any of the aforesaid goods will amount to violation of our clients' rights in their above mentioned trademark. Such use will also amount to infringement of our clients' common law and statutory rights in the mark **"GOOD MORNING"** for which, the infringer will be liable for civil and/or criminal proceedings which may result in jail sentence as well as fine. Our clients have already initiated legal action against violation of their rights in the said trademark. Manufacturers, distributors, dealers, stockists and retailers of the aforesaid goods are also warned against violation of our clients' aforesaid trademark.

R.K. DEWAN & CO.
Trade Marks & Patents Attorneys
Podar Chambers, S.A. Brelvi Road, Fort
Mumbai-400001

Source: *Times of India*, 10 June 2006.

Figure 5.2 Trade Mark Notice.

5.13 REMEDIES AGAINST TRADE MARK INFRINGEMENT

Trade Mark, along with the copyright, is the most sensitive IPR. Since the infringement of these IPR is quite easy, Trade Mark and copyright violation attract both civil and criminal proceedings. The suits for infringements of trade marks are initially filed in District court. The relief against trade mark infringement includes:

5.13.1 Injunction

Whenever the Trade Mark proprietor finds that a third party is using the Trade

Mark in unauthorized way through deception or otherwise, it may approach the court. The court on the basis of prima facie evidence may issue an injunction order restraining the third part from continuing with wrongful act. This is a form of immediate relief for the trade mark proprietor. It restrains the third party from doing any further damage till the final court judgement is given after hearing of both the parties. In case the trade mark proprietor wins the case it may be changed from temporary injunction to perpetual injunction.

As per Section 135 of The Trade Marks Act, 1999 "the order of injunction may include an ex parte injunction or any interlocutory order for any of the following matters, namely:

(a) For discovery of documents
(b) Preserving of infringing goods, documents or other evidence which are related to the subject-matter of the suit
(c) Restraining the defendant from disposing of or dealing with his assets in a manner which may adversely affect plaintiff's ability to recover damages, costs or other pecuniary remedies which may be finally awarded to the plaintiff".[2]

5.13.2 Damages

The court may grant either damages or an account of profit to the trademark proprietor. In case of damages, the court may fix any amount of damages as it deems fit to be paid by the infringer. The damages may be less or more than the profit that the infringer has accumulated due to the infringement. The amount of damages fixed by the court depends on the loss that the infringement brought to the business of trade mark proprietor, directly and indirectly.

5.13.3 Account of Profit

In case of account of profits, the court directs the infringer to pay back the profits accrued to him due to the infringement to the trade mark proprietor. The profit earned by the infringer because of the infringement, and not the entire damage done to the business in the long term, is taken into consideration while calculating the account of profit.

However, all the above remedies are subject to discretion of court. The court may also initiate criminal proceedings against the infringer depending on the extent of severity of violation. The onus to prove the extent of trade mark violation and amount of damages due to the trade mark infringement is on the trade mark proprietor.

---

2. http://www.ipindia.nic.in

5.14 APPELLATE BOARD

An Intellectual Property Appellate Board has been set up on 15 September 2003, with its headquarter at Chennai, and its benches at Mumbai, Delhi, Calcutta and Ahmedabad. It has Chairman, Vice-Chairman and members. The Chairman should be serving Judge of High Court or had been a Judge of the High Court or had for at least two years held the office of a Vice-Chairman. The Chairman, Vice-Chairman and members are appointed by the President of India. As per Section 91 of The Trade Marks Act, 1999 any person aggrieved by an order or decision of the Registrar of Trade Marks or rules made thereunder may prefer an appeal to the Appellate Board within three months from the date on which the order or decision sought to be appealed against is communicated to such person preferring the appeal.

The Appellate Board is not bound by the procedures laid down in the Code of Civil Procedure, 1908 but it is guided by principles of natural justice. The Appellate Board has the powers to regulate its own procedure including the fixing of places and times of its hearing. The proceedings before Appellate Board have judicial sanctity and it has powers equivalent to Civil Court. All the cases of appeals against any order or decision of the Registrar and all cases pertaining to rectification of register of trade marks, pending before any High Court, were transferred to Appellate Board.

5.15 CYBERSQUATTING AND TRADE MARKS

The internet has become pervasive across homes, offices and businesses. The importance of presence of businesses on internet is increasing as all stakeholders including consumers are accessing internet for different kind of organizational information. With this rise in usage and relevance of internet, the phenomenon of cybersquatting had also been on the rise. Cybersquatting involves registering various domain names including those similar to renowned organizations in one's name with the intention to sell it to the interested parties at profit. The domain name registration under cybersquatting is done with a motive to negatively leverage it due to high goodwill of trade mark in the market place. The domain names have got commercial implications as they are related to its trade mark and may confuse the prospective consumers and other trade partners. The main intention of cyber squatters is to sell these domain names to their original owners whose organization name or its part is there in the registered domain name at inflated price making huge profits.

In order to check this menace which is quite prevalent across countries, WIPO (World Intellectual Property Organization), ICANN (Internet Corporation for Assigned Names and Numbers) and each country had made additional arrangements to check and resolve this problem. WIPO Arbitration and Mediation Center registers and resolves cybersquatting complains as per Uniform Domain-Name Dispute-Resolution Policy (UDRP) developed by ICANN, the global body that coordinates the entire internet system. According to WIPO website, it registered 2696 cybersquatting cases covering 4370 domain names in 2010, filed by different trade mark owners. USA has enacted a law in 1999 viz. Anticybersquatting Consumer Protection Act (ACPA) to check cybersquatting involving trade mark of various US companies. In India, provisions against cybersquatting are made in Trade Marks Act, 1999; Information Technology Act, 2000 and the court rulings in similar cases. Besides legal provisions, awareness and initiatives regarding protection against cybersquatting amongst commercial enterprises is best cure for this menace.

5.16 SUMMARY

Trade Mark is defined as a mark capable of being represented graphically and which is capable of distinguishing the goods or services of one person from those of others and may include shape of goods, their packaging and combination of colours. It is used to convey origin, quality and product differentiation. Customers are ready to pay a premium for established Trade Marks. The nomenclature and colour scheme of the Trade Mark should ensure that it is new and fresh. This will help the Trade Mark to stand out of the clutter and deter its violation. At times, coining totally new words, that are not part of any dictionary, also gives unique visibility to the Trade Mark. Trade Mark is granted for all things except certain exceptions given under absolute and relative ground of refusal of Trade Mark in The Trade Marks Act, 1999. There is a step wise procedure for grant of Trade Mark. Once Trade Mark is granted the name of proprietor (owner) along with their addresses; notifications of assignment and transmissions; and the names, addresses and descriptions of registered users are entered in Register of Trade Marks. The registration of Trade Mark is for a period of 10 years, but it may be renewed from time-to-time in accordance with the The Trade Marks Act, 1999. Practically the trade mark is for unlimited period of time. The registered proprietor of trade mark, whose name appears in the register of trade marks, has the power to assign or transmit the Trade Mark for any consideration. Trade Mark is a territorial right. However, under Madrid system, the owner of the Trade Mark may get Trade Mark protected in all the Madrid Agreement signatory countries through one application form with his own national Trade Mark office. Trade Mark infringement attracts both civil and criminal proceedings. A Trade Mark is said to be infringed by a person who, not being a registered proprietor, uses in the course of trade, a mark which is identical with, or deceptively similar to, the Trade Mark in relation to good or services in respect of which the Trade Mark is registered and in such manner as to render the use of the mark likely to be taken as being used as a Trade Mark. The remedy against Trade Mark infringement includes injunction, damages and account of profits. The Trade Marks Act, 1999 also provides for an Appellate Board where any person aggrieved by an order or decision of the Registrar of Trade Marks or rules made thereunder, may file an appeal before it. Cybersquatting of trade marks has also been on the rise and various steps have been taken by regulatory bodies to check and resolve it. However, awareness and initiatives regarding protection against cybersquatting amongst commercial enterprises seems to be the best solution to this growing global problem.

CASE STUDY—L'OREAL TRADE MARK DISPUTE

In 18 September 2009, L'Oreal started an intensive advertisement campaign of its 'Fuel' men's skincare brand. The advertisement created a controversy landing L'Oreal in court. L'Oreal is a leading global player in cosmetics products, based in Paris. VLCC is India's leading wellness and cosmetic company which has filed Trade Mark infringement case against L'Oreal. VLCC acquired rights of 'Fuel' Trade Mark from a Delhi based entrepreneur Mahesh Chaudhary, in 2006. Since then VLCC has launched many brand extension products of 'Fuel' like shaving gel, hair styling, after-shave balm, strengthening gel and deodorant. Currently 'Fuel' is around 100 crore brand for VLCC. The L'Oreal claims that they also have bought 'Fuel' Trade Mark right from Mahesh Choudhary in 2009. VLCC has also filed a case against Mahesh Chaudhary for selling the same Trade Mark to L'Oreal. VLCC has threatened that if L'Oreal continues to market 'Fuel' brand further under L'Oreal umbrella then they are going to file another case against L'Oreal. The fight is getting fiercer day-by-day as millions of dollars are on stake as men's skincare market has immense growth potential in India in the near future. This is not the first Trade Mark dispute of L'Oreal. Recently on 22 May 2010, through a court ruling in its favour, L'Oreal has successfully restrained other companies in Europe from marketing similar smelling perfume brands. Presently, the L'Oreal versus VLCC Trade Mark dispute case is sub judice at Delhi High Court. The lawyers from both the parties are also exploring the option of out-of-court settlement.

ISSUES FOR DISCUSSION

1. What remedies for Trade Mark infringement may VLCC get against L'Oreal?
2. What is role of Intellectual Property Appellate Board in case Delhi High Court gives adverse ruling against VLCC?

Discussion Questions

1. What is a Trade Mark? Discuss the important issues to be taken care of while developing a Trade Mark.
2. Explain absolute grounds for refusal of registration of Trade Marks as per The Trade Marks Act, 1999.
3. What is Register of Trade Marks?

4. Discuss relative grounds for refusal of registration of Trade Marks as per The Trade Marks Act, 1999.
5. Elaborate the steps involved in registration of Trade Mark in India.
6. What are various ways of transfer of Trade Mark to a third party?
7. What is Madrid System?
8. Explain what amounts to infringement of Trade Mark as per The Trade Marks Act, 1999.
9. Elaborate the remedies available to the proprietor against Trade Mark infringement.
10. Discuss the relevance and importance of Appellate Board provided under The Trade Marks Act, 1999.

Objective Type Questions

Tick the right answer in given multiple-choice questions:

1. A Trade Mark includes
   (a) Heading (b) Signature (c) Name (d) All of them
2. The term of a Trade Mark is
   (a) 10 years (b) 20 years (c) 30 years (d) 40 years
3. The Mardrid System came into force in
   (a) December, 1995 (b) December, 2000
   (c) December, 2003 (d) December, 2005
4. The most sensitive of all IPRs
   (a) Trade Mark (b) Copyright (c) None of them (d) Both of them
5. The number of days given for public to raise any objection regarding the Trade Mark submitted for registration are:
   (a) 1 month (b) 3 months (c) 5 months (d) 6 months
6. The Appellate Board has powers equivalent to
   (a) Civil Court (b) High Court (c) Supreme Court (d) None of them
7. The remedy against Trade Mark infringement includes
   (a) Injunction (b) Damages (c) Account of Profit (d) All of them
8. The Trade Marks Registry is situated at
   (a) Mumbai (b) Kolkata (c) New Delhi (d) All of them
9. The infringement of Trade Mark attracts
   (a) Civil Suit (b) Criminal Suit (c) None of them (d) Both of them
10. The Chairman of the Appellate Board is appointed by
    (a) Prime Minister of India (b) Chief Justice of India
    (c) President of India (d) None of them

Mark TRUE or FALSE against given statements:

1. The Trade and Merchandise Marks Act, 1958 was the original act governing Trade Marks in India. (True/False)
2. Trade Mark is a territorial right. (True/False)
3. Five months are given to the public to raise any objection regarding the Trade Mark due for the registration. (True/False)
4. The Trade Marks Act, 199 provides only civil remedies against infringement of copyright. (True/False)
5. Trade Marks are used to convey origin, quality and product differentiation. (True/False)

References

Annual Report, Office of Controller General of Patents, Designs, Trade Marks & Geographical Indications, India 2009–2010, Department of Industrial Policy and Promotion, Ministry of Commerce and Industry, Government of India; Available at http://ipindia.gov.in/cgpdtm/AnnualReport_English_2009_2010.pdf

Annual Report, Office of Controller General of Patents, Designs, Trade Marks & Geographical Indications, India 2010–2011, Department of Industrial Policy and Promotion, Ministry of Commerce and Industry, Government of India; Available at http://ipindia.nic.in/cgpdtm/AnnualReport_English_2010_2011.pdf

Annual Report, Office of Controller General of Patents, Designs, Trade Marks & Geographical Indications, India 2011–2012, Department of Industrial Policy and Promotion, Ministry of Commerce and Industry, Government of India; Available at http://ipindia.gov.in/cgpdtm/AnnualReport_English_2011_2012.pdf

Jain, Sneha (2009), "Parallel Imports and Trademark Law", *Journal of Intellectual Property Rights*, Volume 14, pp. 14–27.

Patel, Mayuri and Saha, Subhasis (2008), "Trademark Issues in Digital Era", *Journal of Intellectual Property Rights*, Volume 13, pp. 118–128.

Ramanujan, Adarsh (2008), "Reflections on the Indian Accession to Madrid Protocol", *Journal of Intellectual Property Rights*, Volume 13, pp. 111–117.

Sahay, Shantanu (2006), "Piracy of Trade Dress and the Law Passing off: National and International Perspective", *Journal of Intellectual Property Rights*, Volume 11, pp. 201–206.

Some Questions and Answers on Patents, Copyrights, Designs, Trademarks, IC Layout Designs, Geographical Indications, Patent Facilitating Centre, TIFAC, New Delhi, 2005.

The Trade Marks Act, 1999 Bare Acts, Universal Law Publishing, 2010.

Tomar, Vernika (2009), "Trademark Licensing and Franchising: Trends in Transfer of Rights", *Journal of Intellectual Property Rights*, Volume 14, pp. 397–404.

Websites

http://www.ipindia.nic.in
http://www.wipo.int

CHAPTER 6

Industrial Designs and IC Layout Design

Industrial designs play an important part in shaping customer preference for a product. It helps in creating customer's interest in the product due to the aesthetic appearance. Industrial designs are used for promoting and marketing of products. The Designs Act, 1911 had been replaced with The Designs Act, 2000 to make it contemporary as per current requirements. The new Designs Act, 2000 will help in promoting design activity in products by providing better protection to registered designs. The owner of the industrial design, as per The Designs Act, 2000, is granted a copyright of the design. The industrial designs in India are covered by The Designs Act, 2000 and The Designs Rules, 2001. The design offices are located at Kolkata, Mumbai, Chennai and Delhi.

6.1 INDUSTRIAL DESIGNS

'Design' as per The Designs Act, 2000 means "only the features of shape, configuration, pattern, ornament or composition of lines or colours applied to any article whether in two-dimensional or three-dimensional or in both forms, by any industrial process or means, whether manual, mechanical or chemical, separate or combined, which in the finished article appeal to and are judged solely by eye; but does not include any mode or principle of construction of anything which is in substance a mere mechanical device".[1] The Designs Act, 2000 does not cover the functional aspects of design.

The article in The Designs Act, 2000 means any article of manufacture and any substance, artificial, or partly artificial or partly natural; and includes any part of an article capable of being made and sold separately. Industrial Design is a territorial right, i.e. for protection of copyright of industrial design in different countries one has to apply separately in each country by filing requisite form and fees depending on that country's requirement.

1. http://www.ipindia.nic.in

The examples of Industrial Designs are artistic shape or outward ornamentation of electronic goods, crockery, machine tools, household items, electrical fittings, automobile, musical instruments, footwear, beverage bottles, furniture, medical equipments, etc. The design of iPod and Beetle Car are registered industrial design by Apple and Volkswagen, respectively.

6.2 REGISTRATION OF DESIGNS

The following types of design "are not registrable under The Designs Act, 2000:

(a) A design which is not new or original; or

(b) A design which has been disclosed to the public anywhere in India or in any other country by publication in tangible form or by use or in any other way prior to the filing date, or where applicable, the priority date of the application for registration; or

(c) A design which is not significantly distinguishable from known designs or combination of known designs; or

(d) A design which comprises or contains scandalous or obscene matter".[2]

The Controller-General of Patents, Designs and Trade Marks (CGPDTM) is the Controller of Designs.

6.3 COPYRIGHT IN REGISTERED DESIGNS

Industrial Designs may apply for exclusive copyright under Copyright Act or copyright in designs under The Designs Act, 2000. However, the same product cannot get both. Also a copyright for industrial design would cease to have copyright if copyrighted design is reproduced 50 times by an industrial process by the copyright owner. Therefore, it is better to take copyright in design under The Designs Act, 2000. The Design wing, working under Office of the Controller General of Patents, Designs, Trade Marks and Geographical Indications, received 8373 design applications in 2011–2012 and 6590 copyright for industrial design were issued and registered in that financial year (Table 6.1 and Figure 6.1). Around 5292 design applications were filed from Indian applicants and 3081 applicants were of foreign origin (Table 6.2). Among the design applications which were accepted for registration, 4162 were Indian nationals and 2428 were of foreign origin (Table 6.3). In order to expedite the application processing, electronic processing of all design applications has been introduced since 1 April 2009.

2. http://www.ipindia.nic.in

Table 6.1 Design Applications in India

Year	2004–05	2005–06	2006–07	2007–08	2008–09	2009–10	2010–11	2011–12
Filed	4017	4949	5521	6402	6557	6092	7589	8373
Registered	3728	4175	4250	4928	4772	6025	9206	6590

Source: Annual Report, Office of Controller General of Patents, Designs, Trade Marks & Geographical Indications, India 2009–2010; 2010–2011 and 2011–2012.

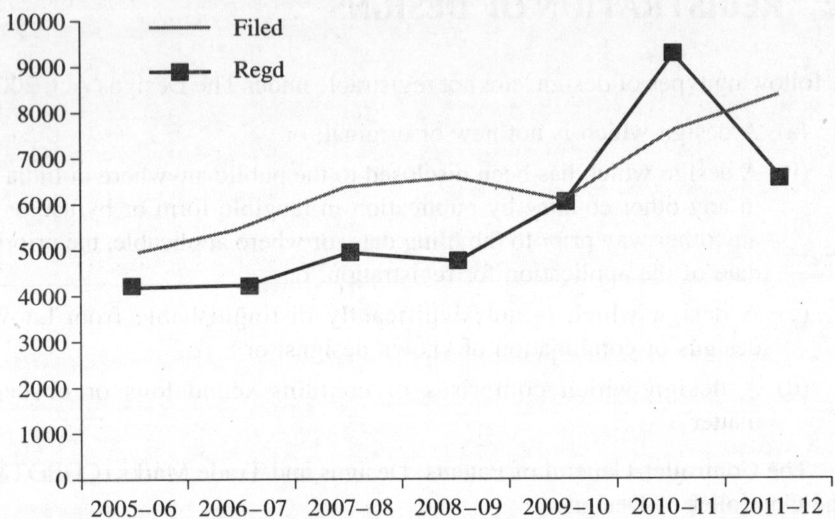

Source: Annual Report, Office of Controller General of Patents, Designs, Trade Marks & Geographical Indications, India 2011–2012.

Figure 6.1 Design Applications in India.

Table 6.2 Trends in Design Applications Filed

Year	2004–05	2005–06	2006–07	2007–08	2008–09	2009–10	2010–11	2011–12
Indian	3093	3407	3584	3873	4308	4267	5095	5292
Foreign	924	1542	1937	2529	2249	1825	2494	3081
Total	4017	4949	5521	6402	6557	6092	7589	8373

Source: Annual Report, Office of Controller General of Patents, Designs, Trade Marks & Geographical Indications, India 2009–2010; 2010–2011 and 2011–2012.

Table 6.3 Trends in Design Applications Registered

Year	2004–05	2005–06	2006–07	2007–08	2008–09	2009–10	2010–11	2011–12
Indian	3166	3439	2877	3026	2985	3552	6369	4162
Foreign	562	736	1373	1902	1787	2473	2837	2428
Total	3728	4175	4250	4928	4772	6025	9206	6590

Source: Annual Report, Office of Controller General of Patents, Designs, Trade Marks & Geographical Indications, India 2009–2010; 2010–2011 and 2011–2012.

6.4 CONDITIONS FOR REGISTRATION OF INDUSTRIAL DESIGNS

The essential conditions for registration of industrial designs as per The Designs Act, 2000 are:

(a) The industrial design should be novel. The novelty may be in the application of a known shape or pattern to new subject matter.
(b) The design should relate to features of shape, configuration, pattern or ornamentation applied or applicable to an article.
(c) The design should be applied or applicable to any article by any industrial process.
(d) The features of the designs in the finished article should appeal to and are judged solely by the eye.
(e) Any mode or principle of construction or operation or anything, which in substance is a mere mechanical device, would not qualify for registrable design.
(f) The design should not include any Trade Mark or property mark or artistic works.

6.5 PROCEDURE FOR REGISTRATION OF INDUSTRIAL DESIGNS

The process for registration of industrial design is comparatively simple. The applicant applies for registration of Industrial Designs to the Controller. It contains the representation of the design and brief statement about novelty of the design. The applicant may be any person claiming to be proprietor of any new or original design not previously published in any country and the design is not contrary to public order or morality. After initial verification of application form regarding requisite fee for registration, representation of the design in documented form and completeness of application, a particular number and date is assigned to the application. The Examiner examines and verifies whether the submitted design with the application is registrable as per the conditions laid down in Designs Act, 2000. In case of any objections, it is communicated to the applicant who has to reply within three months from the date of official communication of objection. However, if there is no objection, the particular industrial design is accepted and Controller directs for its registration and publication in the Official Gazette.

If the applicant does not reply to the Controller regarding objections raised by examiner related to the industrial design within three months, the application is deemed to have been withdrawn. In case, s/he gives a reply to the objection and Controller is not satisfied, and therefore, rejects the application; the applicant may appeal in the High Court (Figure 6.2).

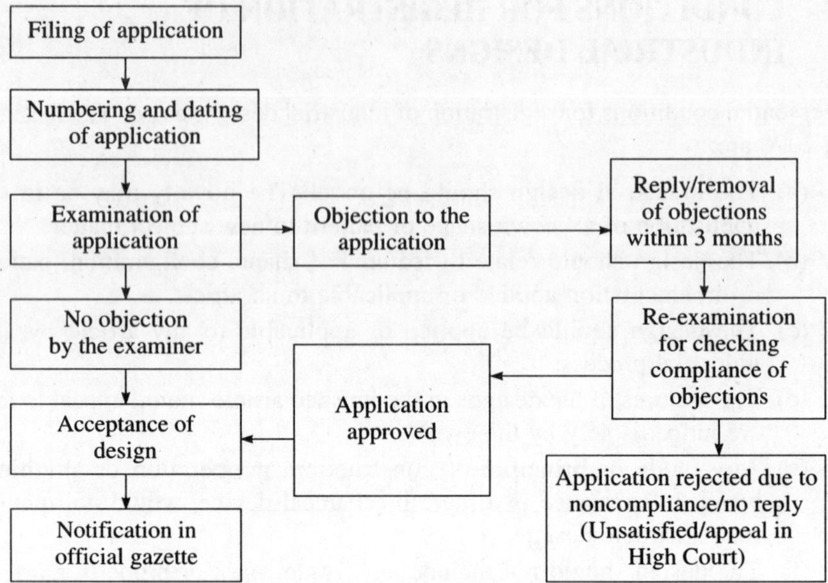

Figure 6.2 Process for Registration of Industrial Designs.

The registration of industrial design of any product is done under a specific class of product. All these classes (about 30) are listed in The Designs Act, 2000. According to Section 5(3) a design may be registered in not more than one class, and in case of doubt as to the class in which a design ought to be registered; the decision of Controller shall be final.

6.6 TERM OF INDUSTRIAL DESIGNS

As per Section 11 of The Designs Act, 2000 when a design is registered, the registered proprietor of the design would get copyright in the design for 10 years from the date of registration. The copyright of design may be extended for another 5 years, in case before 10 years is expired, the request is made to the Controller for extension along with prescribed fee, i.e. the maximum period of copyright of industrial design is 15 years.

In case the extension for copyright of design has not been applied before the expiry of initial 10 years and the copyright has lapsed, then applicant/s may apply within 1 year for the extension of copyright to the Controller. Such application must include statement giving details about circumstances which led to the failure to apply for the extension. The Controller may ask for further evidence as he may think necessary.

6.7 REGISTER OF DESIGNS

The patent office has a book called Register of Designs. It contains names and addresses of owners of registered design; and assignment and transmission details, if any. The Register of Designs may also be maintained wholly or partly on computer floppies or diskettes. The Register of Designs serves as a legal document in case of disputes related to copyright of design. As per Section 29, the Controller, on the written request of applicant, may correct any clerical error in the representation of a design or in the name or address of the proprietor of any design or any other matter in the Register of Designs.

6.8 POWER AND DUTIES OF CONTROLLER

Sections 32 to 36 of The Designs Act, 2000 provides for power and duties of Controller. The Controller has the powers of a civil court. The Controller may use his allocated discretionary power only after giving the applicant an opportunity for hearing or representation. The Controller has the right to refuse the registration of a design if he is of the view that the use of design is against public order or morality.

In case the Controller has doubt or difficulty in interpreting any provisions of the Designs Act, he is free to write to the Central Government for directions in the matter.

6.9 INFRINGEMENT OF INDUSTRIAL DESIGNS

The infringement occurs if during the period of existence of copyright of industrial design anyone does the following without the licence or written consent of the registered proprietor:

(a) Any imitation of the registered design in the product for sale or any related application.

(b) To import for the purposes of sale any article belonging to the class in which the design is registered.

(c) Any imitation applied to any article in any class of articles in which the design is registered; or to publish for sale of that article.

In case any company feels that its industrial design may be violated, it may issue caution notice in newspaper or any other media. This besides providing deterrence against infringement of industrial design also strengthens the industrial design claim of the caution issuing party in case of legal dispute. For Example, SSL-TTK Limited issued caution notice in leading newspaper against any future violation of its trade mark and industrial design (Figure 6.3). The infringement of industrial design is called piracy of registered design as per Section 22 of The Designs Act, 2000.

The onus of identifying or monitoring the infringement of copyright of industrial design lies with the owner of the registered design. S/he needs to keep an eye on any infringement in the form of imitation or fraudulent usage of the registered design and then initiate appropriate steps accordingly if any infringement is seen. The services of Intellectual Property Attorney may also be taken to claim against the infringement in the court.

Trade Mark and Industrial Design Caution Notice

Notice is hereby given that our clients SSL-TTK Limited, a Company incorporated under the Companies Act, 1956 having office at No. 6, Cathedral Road, Chennai-600086, are the managers and administrators in India of all Intellectual Property Rights in the Trademarks "SCHOLL", "DR. SCHOLL'S" and "MASSAGIO" and Industrial Design for footwear bearing design registration number 176333 deriving required authority for the same from Scholl plc, UK, the owners thereof.

Our clients are, inter alia, engaged in the business of manufacture, sourcing, distributing and marketing footwear and foot care products and have been using the said trade marks and design for decades. By virtue of the long and continuous use of the said trade marks and design on footwear, they have become distinctive and have been exclusively associated with our clients and their products.

In order to obtain further statutory protection, the trade marks "SCHOLL", "DR. SCHOLL'S" have been registered and application for registration of the trade mark "MASSAGIO" is pending registration in class 25.

This public notice is issued herein to warm and/or deter all those who are using or intend to use the said trade marks or their artistic labels or of any marks identical or deceptively similar thereto and the said design would constitute on infringement, falsification, piracy, violation of our clients' rights and would entail civil and criminal liability. In such case, our clients shall, at their option, institute appropriate legal proceedings against such case, our clients shall, at their option, institute appropriate legal proceedings against such person(s), including criminal action.

The purchasers and consumers are hereby requested to bring to the notice of our clients instances of such illegal acts and inducement and to identify our clients' original goods with the above-depicted trade marks and industrial design.

Date: 12-06-2006

For Mandal & Associates
Attorneys for SSL-TTK Limited

MASSAGIO

Source: *Times of India*, 12 June 2006.

Figure 6.3 Industrial Design Caution Notice.

6.10 REMEDIES AGAINST INFRINGEMENT OF INDUSTRIAL DESIGNS

The infringement of industrial design attracts civil proceedings. The criminal proceedings are provided only in cases of copyright, IC layout design and Trade Mark violation (Table 6.4). The civil remedies against infringement of industrial design are injunction, damages and confiscation of infringing articles. The injunction provides immediate relief against the violation by restricting the manufacturing and marketing of the said product with immediate effect by the other party against whom the order has been issued. The law also provides for confiscation of infringing articles so as to stop further design violation and deter such offences. According to Section 22(2), a compensation of 25,000 rupees is to be paid to the registered proprietor in case the violation of copyright of design is proved. The proprietor has right to ask for higher damages. The total damages in respect of any one design will not exceed 50,000 rupees.

Table 6.4 Temporal and Spatial Dimensions of IPR

IPR	*Time Period*	*Area of Validity*	*Infringement Proceedings*
Patent	20 years	Country Specific	Civil Proceedings
Copyright	Lifetime + 60 years	Almost Universal	Civil and Criminal Proceedings
Trade Marks	Forever (Renewal after every 10 years)	Country Specific	Civil and Criminal Proceedings
Industrial Design	15 years	Country Specific	Civil Proceedings
Integrated Circuits (IC) Layout Design	10 years	Country Specific	Civil and Criminal Proceedings

6.11 HAGUE AGREEMENT

The registration of copyright in industrial design is a territorial right, i.e. the copyright for the industrial design has to be filed in each country separately wherever the owner of industrial design wants to use it. The Hague System for International Registration of Industrial Designs popularly called as Hague Agreement provides for registration of copyright in industrial design in many countries through filing of a single application. It is similar to what PCT is to Patent and Madrid Agreement is to Trade Marks.

The Hague Agreement enables that the owner of industrial design receives the copyright in industrial design by filing a single application form in any one language with a single set of fees in select or all member nation countries at one go. The registration has the same effect in the respective member countries as it has through direct registration in that member nation. There are presently 38 nations signatory to the Hague Agreement. India is presently not a member of Hague System for International Registration of Industrial Designs.

6.12 INTEGRATED CIRCUITS (IC) LAYOUT DESIGN

The Semiconductor Integrated Circuits (IC) Layout Design Act, 2000 and The Semiconductor Integrated Circuits Layout-Design Rules, 2001 "provides protection for semiconductor IC layout designs. According to the Act the Layout design includes a layout of transistors and other circuitry elements and includes lead wires connecting such elements and expressed in any manner in a semiconductor IC". The size and processing power of IC is dependent on layout design of transistors. The criteria for registration of an IC layout design is that it should be original; not commercially exploited anywhere in India; and distinctive and capable of being distinguishable from any other registered layout design. However, the IC Layout Design Act, 2000 does not provide protection or registration of an idea related to IC layout, programme stored in the IC, procedure, method of operation, etc. The term of an IC layout design protection is 10 years from the date of filing an application for registration.

6.12.1 Grant of Registration of IC Layout Design

The registration for IC layout design is done at Semiconductor Integrated Circuits Layout Design Registry (SICLDR), New Delhi. SICLDR became operational since 1 May 2011. The application is advertized within 14 days of acceptance. Three months time is given for anyone to raise objection against the IC layout design. Any objection raised has to be replied within two months by the applicant. The Registrar may conduct hearing of both the parties and then take a decision on the grant of registration of IC layout design. The Registrar has powers of a civil court. He also has power to refer the case to Layout Design Appellate Board.

Like other IPR offices, the Semiconductor Integrated Circuits Layout Design Registry, New Delhi has Register of Layout Designs. It contains details of registered layout design, names, addresses and description of the proprietor. The Register of Layout Designs is open for public scrutiny on payment of fees.

The Semiconductor Integrated Circuits (IC) Layout Design Act, 2000 provides for civil and criminal proceedings against infringement of registered semiconductor IC layout designs. The application fee for IC layout design application and registration is about rupees six thousand.

6.13 TRADE SECRETS

An innovator has got two choices once s/he invents any product. S/he may file for a patent or go for a trade secret. The patent protection provides protection of the innovation for 20 years. After the expiry of the 20 years period, anyone may manufacture the product or use the technology. In case of trade secret, there is no registration process involved. It can remain as a trade secret forever. However, the onus to protect one's trade secret lies with the owner of the innovation. For example, Coca Cola's formula is a trade secret. No one except the owners know the exact formula for Coca Cola concentrate from which the soft drinks are made. Coca Cola choose not to go for patent instead it opted for maintaining it as a trade secret.

In the modern world with internet, mobile, video, pendrives, scanners, photocopiers, etc. and employees shifting companies quite often; the trade secrets are generally not a preferred option among the organizations. The trade secret option may be opted only in cases where reverse engineering is quite tough; product life cycle is small (as grant of patent takes time) and it is easy to maintain the secret. Each patent begins its life as a trade secret as till the date of filing of patent, the innovation is a closely guarded secret.

The inventor may opt for any innovation to be a trade secret. The greatest temptation or incentive for opting for trade secrets is that it is there for an infinite period of time. However, the protection of the trade secret should be done with utmost safeguard and foolproof manner. Any disclosure in public will mark the death of that particular trade secret. There are no international treaties for the protection of trade secrets or for providing damages against infringements of trade secrets.

6.14 SUMMARY

The Designs Act, 2000 provides protection to industrial designs. The design means the features of shape, configuration, pattern, ornament or composition of lines or colours applied to any article by any industrial process. The industrial designs are judged solely by the eye. The term of industrial designs is 15 years. The Designs Act, 2000 has provision for Register of Designs which maintains the names and addresses of proprietors of registered designs, notifications of assignments and of transmissions of registered designs. It serves as an important legal document in case of disputes. The Controller-General of Patents, Designs and Trade Marks is the Controller of Designs. The Controller has the powers equivalent to civil court. The civil remedies against infringement of industrial design include injunction, damages and confiscation of infringing articles. The Hague System for International Registration of Industrial Designs popularly called as Hague Agreement provides for registration of copyright in industrial design in many countries through filing of a single application. The Semiconductor Integrated Circuits (IC) Layout-Design Act, 2000 and The Semiconductor Integrated Circuits Layout-Design Rules, 2001 provides protection for semiconductor IC layout designs. Some companies also opt for Trade Secret as a method for IPR protection especially when product life cycle is small and it is easy to maintain the secret.

CASE STUDY—TRACTORS AND FARM EQUIPMENT (TAFE) LIMITED

Tractors and Farm Equipment Limited (TAFE) is a $ 1 billion Indian tractor company. It was established in 1960 and has it's headquarter at Chennai. In 2005, TAFE filed a case against the company named Green Field Farm Equipments Limited for industrial design violation. TAFE was working along with UK based vendor for coming up with an innovatively designed tractor. It was to be branded as 'Hunter'. TAFE in its industrial violation case claimed that one of its ex-employee had pirated the industrial design and the same industrial design is used in Maharaja 3300 tractors being manufactured by Green Field Farm Equipments Limited; of which he is current employee. The owner of Green Field Farm Equipments Limited was the ex-employee's wife. The ex-employee had also stint with UK based vendor of TAFE in the 'Hunter' project while he was serving at TAFE. As a result he was privy to all details of proposed 'Hunter' product including industrial design of 'Hunter'. He resigned from TAFE in October, 2003. His resignation was accepted and he started working with Green Field Farm Equipments Limited. In 2005, Green Field Farm Equipments Limited got registration of Industrial Design for Maharaja 3300 tractor. TAFE came to know that Maharaja 3300 was having industrial design exactly same as proposed product 'Hunter'. TAFE filed injunction proceeding against Green Field Farm Equipments Limited in Madras High Court against product Maharaja 3300 claiming commercialization of Maharaja 3300 is an infringement of its industrial design and also the ex-employee had breached employment contract by disclosing confidential information to a rival company, i.e. Green Field Farm Equipments Limited. The Court on comparison of design found that the design registered by Green Field Farm Equipments Limited for Maharaja 3300 tractor was an imitation of design of 'Hunter' tractor and since the ex-employee was working in the same project it was concluded that it is a case of industrial design violation. The Court in its final verdict ordered injunction on commercialization of Maharaja 3300 tractor with immediate effect. However, it stated that Green Field Farm Equipments Limited was free to manufacture and commercialize tractors of its own design and configuration without infringing the rights of other players in the industry.

ISSUES FOR DISCUSSION

1. Why commercialization of Maharaja 3300 is a violation of industrial design as per The Designs Act, 2000?
2. What is the role of confidential information in such cases with regard to industrial design violation?
3. Enumerate the claims through which TAFE proved in the court that Green Field Farm Equipments Limited had violated its industrial design.

Discussion Questions

1. What do you mean by 'Designs' as per The Designs Act, 2000?
2. Give examples of industrial designs.

3. Elaborate the conditions for registration of Industrial Designs in India.
4. Discuss the power and duties of Controller.
5. What is Hague Agreement?
6. Explain spatial and temporal dimensions of IPR with special reference to industrial designs.
7. What are the steps involved in grant of registration of IC Layout Design?
8. Explain what amounts to infringement of industrial designs as per The Designs Act, 2000.
9. Elaborate the remedies available to the proprietor against infringement of industrial designs.
10. What is a Trade Secret? What are conditions when trade secret is a better option than patent?

Objective Type Questions

Tick the right answer in given multiple-choice questions:

1. An Industrial Design includes
   (a) Configuration (b) Pattern (c) Ornamentations (d) All of them
2. The term of an Industrial Design is
   (a) 10 years (b) 15 years (c) 20 years (d) 40 years
3. The term of an IC layout design protection is
   (a) 10 years (b) 15 years (c) 20 years (d) 40 years
4. Coca Cola is a classic example of
   (a) Patent (b) Trade Secret (c) None of them (d) Both of them
5. The number of days given within which the application for IC layout design is advertized, is:
   (a) 14 days (b) 15 days (c) 20 days (d) 30 days
6. The Controller has powers equivalent to
   (a) Civil Court (b) High Court (c) Supreme Court (d) None of them
7. The remedy against industrial designs infringement includes
   (a) Injunction (b) Damages (c) Confiscation of infringing articles
   (d) All of them
8. The Semiconductor Integrated Circuits Layout Design Registry is situated at
   (a) Mumbai (b) Kolkata (c) New Delhi (d) All of them
9. The infringement of industrial designs attracts
   (a) Civil Suit (b) Criminal Suit (c) None of them (d) Both of them
10. Trade Secret is valid for
    (a) 10 years (b) 15 years (c) 20 years (d) Infinite Period of Time

Mark TRUE or FALSE against given statements:

1. The Designs Act, 2000 does not cover the functional aspects of design. (True/False)
2. Industrial Designs is a territorial right. (True/False)
3. The Controller-General of Patents, Designs and Trade Marks is the Controller of Designs. (True/False)
4. The Designs Act, 2000 provides only criminal remedies against infringement of industrial designs. (True/False)
5. The Semiconductor Integrated Circuits (IC) Layout-Design Act, 2000 and The Semiconductor Integrated Circuits Layout-Design Rules, 2001 provides protection for semiconductor IC layout designs. (True/False)

References

Annual Report, Office of Controller General of Patents, Designs, Trade Marks & Geographical Indications, India 2009-10, Department of Industrial Policy and Promotion, Ministry of Commerce and Industry, Government of India; Available at http://ipindia.gov.in/cgpdtm/AnnualReport_English_2009_2010.pdf

Annual Report, Office of Controller General of Patents, Designs, Trade Marks & Geographical Indications, India 2010–2011, Department of Industrial Policy and Promotion, Ministry of Commerce and Industry, Government of India; Available at http://ipindia.nic.in/cgpdtm/AnnualReport_English_2010_2011.pdf

Annual Report, Office of Controller General of Patents, Designs, Trade Marks & Geographical Indications, India 2011–2012, Department of Industrial Policy and Promotion, Ministry of Commerce and Industry, Government of India; Available at http://ipindia.gov.in/cgpdtm/AnnualReport_English_2011_2012.pdf

Harshwardhan and Keshri, Saurav (2008), "Trade Secrets: A Secret Still to Unveil", *Journal of Intellectual Property Rights*, Volume 13, pp. 208–217.

Some Questions and Answers on Patents, Copyrights, Designs, Trademarks, IC Layout Designs, Geographical Indications, Patent Facilitating Centre, TIFAC, New Delhi, 2005.

The Designs Act, 2000 Bare Acts along with The Designs Rules, 2001, Universal Law Publishing, 2010.

The Times of India, 12 June 2006; Industrial Design Caution Notice Advertisement.

Websites

http://www.ipindia.nic.in

http://www.nopr.niscair.res.in/bitstream/.../1/JIPR%2011(5)%20359-363.pdf

http://www.patentoffice.nic.in/ipr/design/Design_RegistrationBooklet/Registration Booklet_05February2010.pdf

http://www.wipo.int

CHAPTER 7

Geographical Indications

Geographical Indications (GIs) have emerged as major intellectual property asset for protecting consumers' interest and providing recognition to the high and distinct quality local products in the recent times. GIs are used for depicting and securing a link between product quality and a geographical origin. Although GIs have been a part of intellectual property assets kitty for a long period, but widespread awakening of their business value has brought them in the category of consciously pursued business asset. Especially, in case of developing countries GIs are being used for associating products with their places of origin and exploring external markets for the protected local products. Apart from having business value GIs are also being visualized as a tool for protecting traditional knowledge and ushering in development for the places of origin.

7.1 UNDERSTANDING THE CONCEPT OF GEOGRAPHICAL INDICATIONS

Goods originating from a particular geographical place may attain a reputation out of their distinct quality, aesthetics or other characteristics. Because of this reputation, these goods are expected to create a niche market and command a premium price in the marketplace. Availability of premium price and consumer preference may lead to flow of goods in the market place containing false indication of geographical origin. Goods bearing false indication claim to be originating from the specific geographical place contrary to the reality. Goods carrying false indications may provide competition to the goods actually originating from the specific geographical place, and can lead to erosion of reputation of the goods, because of not carrying the quality or characteristics associated with the specific geographical place.

There are a number of terms demanding a distinction for understanding the concept of GIs. These terms include 'Indication of Source', 'Appellations of Origin' and 'Geographical Indications'. Firstly, 'Indication of Origin' can be put forward as a broad concept including any indication pointing directly or indirectly to a place of origin or country without a requirement that a particular reputation, quality or characteristic follows from the origin. This can be termed as 'made in …' type of tag. On the other end, 'Appellations of Origin' is a narrow concept in line with Article 2(1) of the Lisbon Agreement. 'Appellations of Origin' means the geographical name of a country, region, or locality, which serves to designate a product originating therein, the quality and characteristics of which are due exclusively or essentially to the geographical environment, including natural and human factors. Finally, Article 22(1) of TRIPS Agreement states that Geographical Indications are indications which identify a good as originating in the territory of a Member, or a region or locality in that territory, where a given quality, reputation or other characteristic of the good is essentially attributable to its geographical origin. Definition of GIs as provided by TRIPS Agreement is less strict as compared to definition of 'Appellations of Origin' provided by Lisbon agreement. Firstly, as per TRIPS an indication can be other than geographical name of a country, region and locality. Although, most of the GIs contain geographical name of a country, region and locality, such as Canadian Rye Whisky, Real California Cheese, Mysore Silk, and so on, yet exceptions can be there. For example, '*basmati*' although indicating that it originates from India sub-continent, but it is not a name of a geographical place. Secondly, the link between quality and characteristics of the product and geographical place has been toned down from "due exclusively" in case of Lisbon Agreement to "attributable" in TRIPS.

7.2 HISTORICAL PERSPECTIVE ON GEOGRAPHICAL INDICATIONS

Paris Convention of 20 March 1883, for the Protection of Industrial Property was the first attempt in terms of international framework to grant protection for the indicators of the geographical origin for the goods. Paris convention resulted in protecting the indications of source and appellations of origin, but fell short of stipulating any particular requirement relating to reputation, quality or characteristic of the product. Major focus of Paris convention was on the source of the product while ignoring the features of the product.

Madrid Agreement of 14 April 1891, for the Repression of False or Deceptive Indications of Source on Goods attempted to address the issue of "deceptive indications of the goods". "Deceptive indications of the goods" represent a situation where indications are literally true, but different from the origin perceived by the consumers. For example, two cities from two different countries can have the same name and although indication perceived by the consumers may pertain to only one city yet the goods originating from the other may use the indication in a deceptive manner. Both Paris convention and Madrid Agreement contain provisions for remedies and seizure in case of false indications.

Lisbon Agreement for the Protection of Appellations of Origin and their International Registration of 31 October 1958, provided the definitions of notion of Appellation of Origin and Country of Origin along with the provision of registration of appellations of origin with an international bureau. Subsequently, GIs were made a part of TRIPS Agreement under WTO.

7.3 POTENTIAL BENEFITS OF GEOGRAPHICAL INDICATIONS

There are a number of potential benefits associated with GIs. Major benefits of GIs have been listed as follows:

- GIs can be helpful in establishing a niche for the product in national and international markets.
- GIs help in getting a premium price for the producers.
- GIs are instrumental in informing the consumers about the true origin of the product and prevent the consumers from being misled or cheated.
- GIs protect indigenous knowledge and methods of production.
- Joint efforts of members of producer association can be instrumental in reducing cost and improving the quality.
- GIs can be used as a tool for socio-economic development for the specific geographical area from where the goods originate.

7.4 DEFINITION OF GEOGRAPHICAL INDICATION

Section 1(3)(e) of The Geographical Indications of Goods (Registration and Protection) Act,1999 sates that, "Geographical Indication", in relation to goods, means an indication which identifies such goods as agricultural goods, natural goods or manufactured goods as originating, or manufactured in the territory of a country, or a region or locality in that territory, where a given quality, reputation or other characteristic of such goods is essentially attributable to its geographical origin, and in case where such goods are manufactured goods one of the activities of either the production or of processing or preparation of the goods concerned takes place in such territory, region or locality, as the case may be.

For the purpose of the definition given above, goods means any agricultural, natural or manufactured goods or any goods of handicraft or of industry and includes food stuff. "Indication" includes any name, geographical or figurative representation or any combination of them conveying or suggesting the geographical origin of goods to which it applies.

7.5 GEOGRAPHICAL INDICATION IN INDIA

Chapter II of The Geographical Indications of Goods (Registration and

Protection) Act, 1999 deals with the register and conditions for registration of GIs. Section 3(1) of the Act states that The Controller-General of Patents, Designs and Trade Marks appointed under sub-section (1) of Section 3 of the Trade Marks Act, 1999, shall be the Registrar of Geographical Indications. Section 6(1) provides for a Register of GIs to be kept at the Head Office of the Geographical Indications Registry. This register contains all registered geographical indications with the names, addresses and descriptions of the proprietors, the names, addresses and descriptions of authorized users and such other matters relating to registered geographical indications. As per Section 7(1) this register has been divided into two parts, i.e. Part A and Part B. Part A contains the particulars relating to the registration of the geographical indications, while Part B contains the particulars relating to the registration of the authorized users. As per the provisions of the act, registration of GI and the registration of authorized users are recorded separately in the GI registry.

7.5.1 Prohibition of Registration of Certain Geographical Indications

As per The Geographical Indications of Goods (Registration and Protection) Act, 1999, the following GIs cannot be registered:

- The use of which would be likely to deceive or cause confusion
- The use of which would be contrary to any law for the time being in force
- Which comprises or contains scandalous or obscene matter
- Which comprise or contains any matter likely to hurt the religious susceptibilities of any class or section of the citizens of India
- Which would otherwise be disentitled to protection in a court
- Which are determined to be generic names or indications of goods and are, therefore, not or ceased to be protected in their country of origin, or which have fallen into disuse in that country
- Which although literally true as to the territory, region or locality in which the goods originate, but falsely represent to the persons that the goods originate in another territory, region or locality, as the case may be, shall not be registered as a Geographical Indication

7.5.2 Procedure and Duration of Registration

Chapter III of The Geographical Indications of Goods (Registration and Protection) Act, 1999 deals with the procedure of registration and the duration of the registration.

Registration Procedure

As per Section 11(1) of the Act, any association of persons or producers or any organization or authority established by or under any law for the time being in force representing the interest of the producers of the concerned goods, who are desirous of registering a geographical indication in relation to such goods can apply for the registration of GI. For registering GI, an application in writing is made, by any of the parties mentioned above, to the Registrar along with the payment of the prescribed fee.

An application in triplicate to this effect can be made to the following address in India:

Geographical Indications Registry
Intellectual Property Office Building
Industrial Estate, G.S.T. Road
Guindy, Chennai-600032

7.5.3 Content of Application for Registration of a Geographical Indication

Rule 32(1) of The Geographical Indications of Goods (Registration and Protection) Rules, 2002 deals with the content of the application for registering a GI. As per the rule, every application for the registration of a Geographical Indication shall be made in the prescribed forms and shall contain the following:

(a) A statement as to how the Geographical Indication serves to designate the goods as originating from the concerned territory of the country or region or locality in the country, as the case may be, in respect of specific quality, reputation or other characteristics which are due exclusively or essentially to the geographical environment, with its inherent natural and human factors, and the production, processing or preparation of which takes place in such territory, region or locality.

(b) The class of goods to which the Geographical Indication relates shall apply.

(c) The geographical map of the territory of the country or region or locality in the country in which the goods are produced of originate or are being manufactured.

(d) The particulars regarding the appearance of the Geographical Indication as to whether it comprises the words or figurative elements or both.

(e) A statement containing such particulars of the producers of the concerned goods proposed to be initially registered.

(f) The statement contained in the application shall also include the following:

- An affidavit as to how the applicant claim to represent the interest of the association of persons or producers or any organization or authority established by or under any law.
- The standards benchmark for the use of the Geographical Indication or the industry standard as regards the production, exploitation, making or manufacture of the goods having specific quality, reputation, or other characteristic of such goods that is essentially attributable to its geographical origin. (Along with the detailed description of the human creativity involved, if any or other characteristic from the definite territory of the country, region or locality in the country).
- The particulars of the mechanism to ensure that the standards, quality, integrity and consistency or other special characteristic in respect of the goods to which the Geographical Indication relates which are maintained by the producers, maker or manufacturers of the goods.
- Three certified copies of the map of the territory, region or locality showing the title, name of publisher and date of issue along with the application.
- The particulars of special human skill involved or the uniqueness of the geographical environment or other inherent characteristics associated with the Geographical Indication to which the application relates.
- The full name and address of the association of persons or organization or authority representing the interest of the producers of the concerned goods.
- The particulars of the inspection structure, if any, to regulate the use of the Geographical Indication in respect of the goods for which application is made in the definite territory region or locality mentioned in the application.

7.5.4 Registration Process of Geographical Indication in India

Process for registering Geographical Indication in India is being discussed in the following section. The registration process has been depicted in Figure 7.1.

7.5.5 Examination of the Application

After receiving the application, the Registrar examines the application and the accompanying Statement of Case as required under rule 32(1) as to whether it meets the requirements of the Act and the Rules. For this purpose, a consultative group, chaired by the Registrar, is constituted. Consultative group can consist of not more than seven persons from organization or authority or persons well-versed in the varied intricacies of GIs. This consultative group is responsible for ascertaining the correctness of the particulars furnished in the Statement

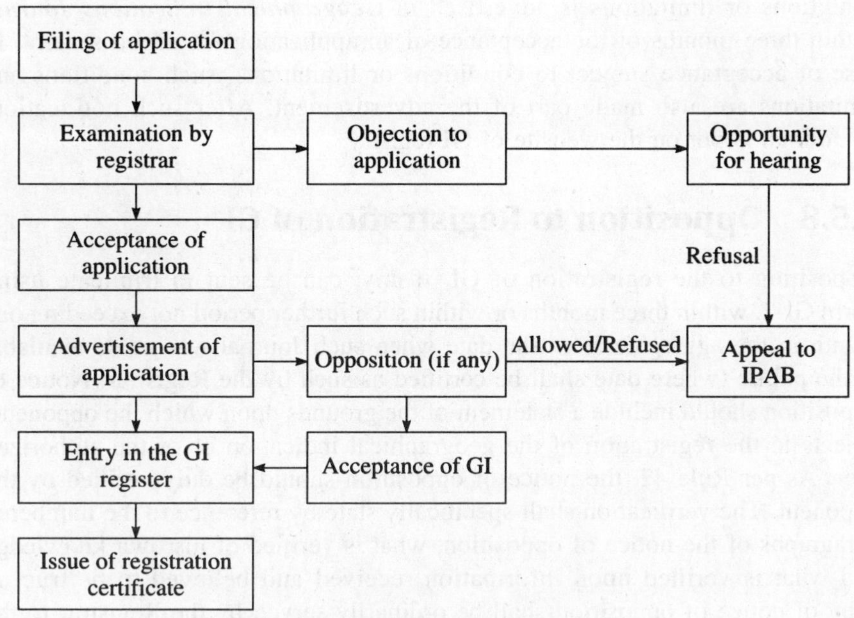

Figure 7.1 Registration Process of GI.

of Case. Consultative group ordinarily completes its job within three months from its date of constitution. Subsequently, the examination report regarding the application is issued to the applicant.

7.5.6 Acceptance of the Application

After considering the application, the Registrar may have objection to the acceptance of application or may propose to accept it subject to some conditions, amendments, modifications or limitations. Such objections/proposals for modification are based on any evidence of use or of a given quality, reputation or other characteristic of such goods that are essentially attributable to its geographical origin. Such objections/proposals are communicated to the applicant. After receiving the communication, the applicant has to amend the application or submit his observations or apply for the hearing within two months of the date of such communication. Inability of the applicant to do so leads to the dismissal of the application.

For making correction and amendments in the application before or after the acceptance of the application, but before the registration of GI, application on Form GI-5 can be made along with the prescribed fee.

7.5.7 Advertisement of Application

After the acceptance of the application whether absolutely of subject to conditions or limitations is advertised in *Geographical Indications Journal* within three months of the acceptance of an application for advertisement. In case of acceptance subject to conditions or limitations, such conditions and limitations are also made part of the advertisement. After such notification, GI Journal is put on the website of GI registry.

7.5.8 Opposition to Registration of GI

Opposition to the registration of GI, if any, can be sent in triplicate using Form GI-2, within three months or within such further period not exceeding one month in the aggregate from the date when such Journal was made available to the public (where date shall be certified as such by the Registrar. Notice of opposition should include a statement of the grounds upon which the opponents objects to the registration of the geographical indication or of the authorized user. As per Rule 42, the notice of opposition should be duly verified by the opponent. The verification shall specifically state by reference to the numbered paragraphs of the notice of opposition, what is verified of his own knowledge and what is verified upon information received and believed to be true. A copy of notice of opposition shall be ordinarily served by the Registrar to the applicants within two months of the receipt of the same.

After receiving the copy of notice of opposition, within two months the applicant is required to send the counter statement on triplicate on Form GI-2 to the registrar. This counter statement should set out the facts if any, alleged in the notice of opposition, are admitted by the applicant. The counter statement provided by the applicant should be verified in line with Rule 42. A copy of the counter-statement is served by the Registrar on the person giving notice of opposition ordinarily within two months from the date of receipt of the same.

Both the parties, the applicant and the opponent are normally given a stipulated period, normally of two months, for submitting the evidence in support of their claims after receiving the communication from the registrar regarding the affidavits of opposition or a copy of counter statement. Upon completion of the evidence (if any), the Registrar gives notice to the parties of a date when he will hear the arguments in the case. Such notices are ordinarily given within three months of completion of the evidence. After receiving the notice of hearing, within fourteen days, the parties are expected to notify the registrar for being interested in the hearing. Otherwise, ex-parte proceedings are undertaken. If both the parties are interested in hearing and appear for the same, the Registrar makes a decisions based on the arguments and evidence provided by the parties.

7.5.9 Entry in the GI Register

If no opposition is received to the advertise application or oppositions are set aside, an enter effecting the registration of GI is made in Part A of the register.

The entry of a geographical indication in the register shall specify the date of filing of application, the actual date of the registration, the goods and the class in respect of which it is registered. Other particulars entered in the register include the name, description and the address of principal place of business in India. Individual or association of persons or producers in whose name the registration is made is termed as the proprietor of GI.

7.5.10 Issue of Registration Certificate

Subsequent to the entry in the GI register, the Registrar issues a certificate to this effect. Duplicate copies of the certificate of registration of a Geographical Indication on request by the registered proprietor on Form GI-7.

7.5.11 Registration as an Authorized User

An application to the Registrar for the registration by a producer as an authorised user of the registered Geographical Indication can be made jointly by the registered proprietor and the proposed authorised user in Form GI-3 and the same is accompanied by a Statement of Case of how he claims to be the producer of the registered Geographical Indication along with an affidavit.

"Producer" in this case means any person who:

- if such goods are agricultural goods, produces the goods and includes the person who processes or packages such good.
- if such goods are natural goods, exploits the goods.
- if such goods are handicraft or industrial goods, makes or manufactures the goods, and includes any person who trades or deals in such production, exploitation, making or manufacturing, as the case may be, of the goods.

Normally, a copy of the letter of consent from the registered proprietor of the Geographical Indication may accompany the application and where such consent letter is not furnished, a copy of the application shall be endorsed to the registered proprietor for information and the Registrar shall be intimated of due service by the proposed authorized user.

After receiving the application, the Registrar examines the application and issues a report. For completing, the registration of an authorized user the same steps are followed as in case of the registration of GI, but for the difference that the details of the authorized users are entered in Part B of the register.

7.6 DURATION AND RENEWAL OF GI

A geographical indication is registered for a period of ten years. Further, the period of protection can be extended by undertaking the renewal process.

Registration of an authorized user is for ten years or till the date on which the registration of the geographical indication expires, whichever is earlier. For example, if an authorized user has registered after two years of registration of geographical indication, then registration of the authorized user will expire after eight years. An application for the renewal of the registration of a Geographical Indication or an authorised user of a registered Geographical Indication can be made on Form GI-4 or Form GI-3 as the case may be and may be made at any time not more than six months before the expiration of the last registration of the Geographical Indication or the authorised user.

7.6.1 Appeal

Any person aggrieved by an order or decision of Registrar may file an appeal to the Intellectual Property Appellate Board (IPAB) within three months. The decision of the Appellate Board is final and binding.

7.7 INFRINGEMENT OF GEOGRAPHICAL INDICATIONS

Section 22(1) of Geographical Indications of Goods (Registration and Protection) Act, 1999 provides that a Geographical Indication can be infringed in the following manner:

- When an unauthorized user uses a Geographical Indication that indicates or suggests that such goods originate in a geographical area other than the true place of origin of such goods in a manner which mislead the public as to the geographical origin of such goods.
- When the use of Geographical Indication results in an unfair competition including passing off in respect of registered Geographical Indication.
- When the use of another Geographical Indication results in false representation to the public that goods originate in a territory in respect of which a registered Geographical Indication relates.

7.8 STATUS OF GI REGISTRATION IN INDIA

Cultural diversity, traditional knowledge and indigenous skills of people in India make India a country from where a large and valuable treasure of Geographical Indications can emanate. After the enactment of act related to Geographical indications in 1999 and subsequently, related rules in 2002, registration activity has picked up. As on 31 October 2013, 462 applications were submitted for registration of Geographical Indication India. Out of these applications, 195 Geographical Indications were registered. Majority of Geographical Indications registered in India relate to handicrafts and agriculture goods commanding a share of 67 percent and 24 percent, respectively. The remaining share belongs to manufactured goods and foodstuff. Few examples of Geographical Indication registered in India include:

- Darjeeling Tea
- Chanderi Fabric
- Kota Doria
- Mysore Agarbatti
- Kangra Tea
- Mysore Sandalwood Oil
- Coorg Orange
- Navara Rice
- Nakshi Kanta

7.9 BENEFITS OF REGISTRATION OF GEOGRAPHICAL INDICATIONS

Benefits of registering a Geographical Indication are listed as follows:

- It confers legal protection to Geographical Indications in India by preventing unauthorized use of a registered Geographical Indication by others.
- It can boost exports of Indian Geographical Indications by providing legal protection.
- Proprietors and authorized users can seek legal protection in other WTO member countries.
- An action for infringement can be initiated only in case of registered Geographical Indication.
- The registered proprietor and authorized users can initiate infringement actions against unauthorized users.
- The authorized users are in a position to exercise the exclusive right to use the Geographical Indication.

7.10 SUMMARY

Geographical Indications have recently gained importance as intellectual property because of their business value. Primary function of a Geographical Indication is to depict and secure link between product quality and a geographical origin. Geographical Indication is a negative right as it prevents non-authorized users to make use of Geographical Indication. Although being an intellectual property a Geographical Indication cannot be assigned, transmitted, licensed, or pledged. Geographical Indications are registered with the GI registry in Chennai for an initial period of ten years and can be renewed afterwards. Registration of a Geographical Indication is done in Part A of the register and registration of authorized users is entered in Part B. Along with the provision of business opportunities in domestic and international markets, Geographical Indications are being viewed as the tools for protecting the traditional knowledge as well as ushering in socio-economic development of the areas acting as the origin for the products.

CASE STUDY—PETRO PRODUCTS FROM JAMNAGAR

Reliance Industries Limited (RIL) had applied for registering five Geographical Indications, i.e., Reliance Jamnagar petrol, Reliance Jamnagar diesel, Reliance Jamnagar LPG (Liquefied Petroleum Gas), Reliance Jamnagar fuel and Krishna Godavari gas in 2004. The consultative group accepted the applications in respect of Reliance Jamnagar petrol, Reliance Jamnagar diesel, Reliance Jamnagar LPG and Reliance Jamnagar fuel after deleting Reliance from the GI name under class 4 of goods that include Petrol, Fuel, LPG and Diesel. The applicant was asked to get no-objection certificate from the petroleum and natural gas ministry regarding the application on Krishna Godavari Gas. Accepted applications were grouped into a single application and were advertised in GI journal with the following specifications:

Jamnagar-Petrol

The Jamnagar manufacturing complex is a largest industrial project set up at a cost of 142.5 billion, fully-integrated manufacturing complex, with (i) petroleum refinery complex, (ii) an aromatics/petrochemical complex, (iii) a power generation complex, (iv) a port and terminal complex, with access to a pipeline network with a Crude Processing Capacity of 27 million metric tonnes per annum. The applicants are the largest producer of Petrol. The Product is used for Automobile Purpulsion for transportation purpose in Internal Combustion Spark Ignition Engines and Lighter Vehicles. This high degree of integration at the Jamnagar complex allows for feedstock and product linkages that will lead to higher efficiencies and enhanced value addition.

Jamnagar-Fuel

It is a propellant used in Aircraft Turbine Engines. The fuel consists wholly of Hydrocarbon compounds derived from conventional source including crude oil, natural gas liquid condensation and qualified additives.

Jamnagar-LPG

The applicants are the largest producer of Liquified Petroleum Gas (LPG). The applicant had stated that the LPG produced is meeting almost 25% of the country's demand. This is a Gaseous product with no odour. It is an inflammable material

Ethyl Mercaptans is added in very small quantity (20 parts per million) to impart it a distinctive smell for detection of this material in case of leakage.

Jamnagar–Diesel

- Diesel primarily used as Transportation Fuel
- Diesel is used in Heavy Vehicles, Railway Engines, Marine Engines, Agricultural Pumps and Power Generation Plants
- This product is now exported leading to increase in Foreign Exchange and Economic Development of the Country

Subsequent to advertisement, four oppositions were received pertaining one each to the four indications. Hearing regarding these oppositions were slated for in July 2009. According to the available news reports, RIL decided to withdraw its four applications regarding the registration of Geographical Indications. Fifth application on Krishna Godavari gas was considered abandoned for the want of no-objection certificate from the concerned ministry.

ISSUES FOR DISCUSSION

1. What type of benefits could have accrued to RIL from the registration of Geographical Indications?
2. What can be the reasons for the reported withdrawal of applications?
3. Do you see any possibility of registration of such Geographical Indications in the future?

Discussion Questions

1. Define Geograhical Indication. Discuss the process of registration of a Geographical Indication.
2. Differentiate "Indication of Source" and "Appellation of Origin".
3. Discuss in detail the evolution of Geographical Indications.
4. What types of Geographical Indications are prohibited for registration on India?
5. Discuss the manner in which a Geographical Indication can be infringed.
6. Elaborate the contents of application for registration of Geographical Indication.
7. Write short notes on the following:
   (a) Uses of Geographical Indication
   (b) Benefits of registering a Geographical Indication
   (c) Opposition to registration of Geographical Indication
8. "TRIPS takes a liberal view of Geographical Indication". Comment on the statement.

Objective Type Questions

Tick the right answer in given multiple-choice questions:

1. The Registry of Geographical Indication in India is at
   (a) New Delhi (b) Kolkata (c) Chennai (d) Mumbai
2. Duration of registration of a Geographical Indication is
   (a) 10 years (b) 15 years (c) 20 years (d) 25 years
3. Registration of a Geographical Indication is done in which part of the register
   (a) Part A (b) Part B (c) Part C (d) Part D
4. Registration of an authorized user is done in which part of the register
   (a) Part A (b) Part B (c) Part C (d) Part D
5. What can be the maximum number of persons in consultative group made for examining the application for registration of Geographical Indication?
   (a) Four (b) Five (c) Six (d) Seven
6. Who is considered as producer in case of a Geographical Indication?
   (a) Trader only (b) Manufacturer only (c) Miner only
   (d) All of these
7. Advertisement of application is done in
   (a) Newspaper (b) GI Journal (c) Radio (d) TV
8. The Geographical Indications of Goods (Registration and Protection) Act came into being in
   (a) 1995 (b) 1997 (c) 1999 (d) 2001
9. Issue of "deceptive indication of goods" was addressed by
   (a) Paris Convention (b) Hague Convention (c) Madrid Agreement
   (d) Doha Round
10. Notion of "Appellation of Origin" was provided by
    (a) Paris Convention (b) Hague Convention (c) Lisbon Agreement
    (d) Doha Round

Mark TRUE or FALSE against given statements:

1. Geographical indication can be registered for services. (True/False)
2. Geographical indication necessarily should contain the name of the place to which it belongs. (True/False)
3. Geographical indication is a negative right. (True/False)
4. Geographical indications can be licensed. (True/False)
5. Geographical indication cannot be renewed. (True/False)

References

The Geographical Indications of Goods (Registration and Protection) Act, 1999, No. 48 of 1999, Ministry of Law, Justice and Company Affairs (Legislative Department) New Delhi.

Ministry of Commerce & Industry (Department of Industrial Policy and Promotion) Notification New Delhi, the 8th march, 2002. The Geographical Indications of Goods (Registration and Protection) Rules, 2002.

Some Questions and Answers on Patents, Copyrights, Designs, Trademarks, IC Layout Designs, Geographical Indications, Patent Facilitating Centre, TIFAC, New Delhi, 2005.

Various Issues of GI Journal.

Website

www.ipindia.nic.in/girindia/

CHAPTER 8

Creating Intellectual Property

Technology and innovation are value drivers in the dynamic environment now days. World is witnessing a shift in the determinants of development from manufacturing to service sector and from capital resources to knowledge resources. Knowledge management and new product creation are expected to become the major determinants of competitive advantage available to knowing organization in the emerging knowledge economies. Intellectual Property Rights are becoming critical resources for survival and growth of modern day enterprises. Intellectual property rights not only affect profitability and business opportunities of a firm but are also instrumental in bringing about industry structure changes, enacting entry barrier and enhancing bargaining power of a firm across the value system.

8.1 NEED FOR CREATING INTELLECTUAL PROPERTY

At enterprise level, intellectual property rights, such as patents, copyrights and trade marks now account for a majority proportion of market capitalization. There is a pertinent need on part of the enterprises to consciously manage the activities related to intellectual property. With emergence of the knowledge economy and rapid technological changes, creation of intellectual property is becoming indispensable for the modern day businesses, even for survival.

Apart from becoming the necessary instrument for survival of the organization, creation of intellectual property is needed on the following counts:

- Wealth creation
- Identity in the marketplace
- Entering in new markets
- Creation of entry barriers
- Strengthening and safeguarding the existing IP
- Shaping industry architecture
- Protecting traditional knowledge

These points are being discussed in detail as follows:

8.1.1 Wealth Creation

Intellectual property is the source of the wealth in the new economy. New IP invariably lead to increased revenue generation, hence, adding to the wealth. By embedding intellectual property in the products and by means of licensing wealth is created for the entrepreneurs, firms and the stockholders. Intellectual property of the business is treated as an important dimension during the valuation of both the existing as well as new business. Benefits from the new knowledge and intellectual property ultimately contribute to the wealth creation for the whole society.

8.1.2 Identity in the Marketplace

Intellectual property, such as trade marks and industrial designs are instrumental in providing a distinct identity to the product offering in the marketplace. Distinct identity from the crowd helps the business sustain its products and services profitably for longer period. This distinct identity also yields increased repurchases and consumer loyalty. Differentiated product offerings based on IP help in commanding a price premium in the market.

8.1.3 Entering into New Markets

Intellectual property is also required for seeking entry into the new markets by offering solutions that are technologically superior or are cost effective to meet the purchasing power of the customers. Intellectual property can help the business deliver the products based on superior performance and make a smooth entry into existing as well as untapped markets.

8.1.4 Creation of Entry Barriers

Intellectual property can also be used as an entry barrier for discouraging the potential rivals to enter in the market place. Business organizations can commercially exploit this advantage by keeping the new aspirants at a bay and enjoy thick profit margins for a longer period. Business organizations can reap monopolist benefits by leveraging intellectual property as effective entry barrier.

8.1.5 Strengthening and Safeguarding the Existing IP

In the present day intellectual property regime, new intellectual property also acts as a tool for strengthening the existing intellectual property portfolio. New intellectual property combined with the existing IP portfolio can enhance the overall portfolio value many times. New IP can also replace the existing IP that is coming to the end of the protection period. Attempts from the competition, customers and suppliers to 'invent around' the existing IP can also be thwarted by getting new IP in place.

8.1.6 Shaping Industry Architecture

If embedded in the industry standards successfully, intellectual property becomes crucial for the setting up and altering the industry standards. Favourable industry standards, such as in the case of telecommunication and software, help to put the business organization into an enviable positions and also provide a platform for IP creation opportunities for the future.

8.1.7 Protecting Traditional Knowledge

Intellectual property, such as Geographical Indication can be used for protecting local and traditional knowledge from misleading and external infringements. Price premium and increased revenue generation helps in better sustenance and conservation of traditional knowledge.

8.2 PROCESS OF DEVELOPMENT OF IP AND KNOWLEDGE

Intellectual property is the creation of human mind and needs, and usually emanates from the ideas. The first step of creation of intellectual property is the wonder of human intellect. Through the process of observation and experimentation, the humans are able to create IP. Creation of IP and knowledge is not necessarily a structured and planned process, as new inventions can occur to human brains, like a flash in the pan. But in the organizational settings, the creation of IP cannot be left at the mercy of chance; therefore there is a need for figuring out the levels/steps that are usually followed in the process of IP creation. The process of creation of new knowledge/intellectual property is being presented as follows:

There are a number of levels in the process developing IP and knowledge. It is not necessary that all instances of IP creation will be following a structured process, still most of the instances, especially in the organizational settings, are expected to contain most of the steps about to be discussed. The steps related to creation of IP and knowledge are being listed as follows:

- Human Thought Process
- Tacit Ideas/Knowledge
- Codification

- Validation/Experimentation
- Explicit Scientific/Business Knowledge
- Scrutiny
- Intellectual Property

8.2.1 Human Thought Process

First step of the creation of IP of course is the ongoing thought process in the human brain. This thought process is concentrated when encountered with a situation involving problem/opportunity. The challenge thrown by a problem/opportunity is instrumental in collecting the past experiences and knowledge for finding a solution to the present situation. At times random thought processes are able to present solutions to the problem situations that are nonexistent for the time being.

8.2.2 Tacit Ideas/Knowledge

Ongoing thought process in the human brain gives birth to ideas and knowledge. Initially these ideas incubate in the human brain and are not shared with the outside world. When incubation is over these ideas are ready to be shared with others. At times, ideas may not go through the complete process of incubation and forcibly move to the next step of codification as in the case raw ideas emanating from brainstorming process.

8.2.3 Codification

At this stage, the tacit ideas are shared with the others through the codification process of articulation/writing. In context of IP creation, this codification is meant only for a small closed group of associates or for purely individual use.

8.2.4 Validation/Experimentation

In the next step attempts are made for the verification of the idea/knowledge through process of scientific experimentation. In the business settings, endorsement by the associates can act as a substitute for experimentation. At the end of this step, the idea/knowledge stands verified and moves on to the next level.

8.2.5 Explicit Scientific/Business Knowledge

Ideas/knowledge that emerge successfully from the crucible of validation/experimentation are termed as the explicit scientific and business knowledge. Such knowledge is useful and can be valuable in a number of ways, if used judiciously.

8.2.6 Scrutiny

Scientific/business knowledge available from the previous step is scrutinized at two levels before being converted into intellectual property. First level of scrutiny, i.e. internal scrutiny is done at the individual level or organizational level. Internal scrutiny usually involves perusing the available knowledge on the basis of its suitability and likelihood to be converted into intellectual property. Organizational interests and cost-benefit analysis play a major role in the outcome of the internal scrutiny. If the outcome of the internal scrutiny is positive and the individual/organization decides to go ahead with seeking protection for the knowledge, the next step is applying to the relevant authority/ office for grant of protection. After application for grant of intellectual property is made, the process of external scrutiny gets underway. External scrutiny involves proceeding with the application as per the established law.

8.2.7 Intellectual Property

If the external scrutiny yields positive result, IP comes into existence and the sought protection is awarded to the applicant. IP thus obtained can be exploited commercially either through licensing or through the sale of products and services developed by the using/embedding IP.

Creation of IP/new knowledge is primarily the output of innovation. Innovation can be defined both as a process and outcome. As process, innovation can be the manner in which a new technology/business solution can be reached at. In form of an outcome, innovation can be defined as a product, service or a new method of production. In fact, IP can also be termed as the outcome of the innovation process.

Innovations come into effect primarily either in the form of market pull innovations or technology push innovations. Market pull innovation are driven by market factors such as the demand from the customers. This type of innovation is driven by the pursuit for finding out solutions to customer needs and account for 60 percent to 80 percent of the total innovations. Use of Hindi language mobile phones and attempts for making the electronic gadgets more customer friendly are the examples of market pull innovations. Technology push innovations on the other hand are the autonomous pursuit of advanced technology by the researchers and the scientists. 3G telecommunication, and High Definition TV are the examples of technology push innovations.

8.3 TYPES OF INNOVATIONS

Any product or process can be viewed as the sum total of specific technologies/ components and the arrangement of theses technologies for building the whole product or process. The arrangement of specific technologies/components is also called component configuration. A new innovation is expected to happen by making changes, either in the specific technologies/components or their composition.

Henderson and Clark (1990) have attempted to classify the innovations on the following two dimensions:

- Degree of departure of specific technologies of an innovation from earlier innovations
- Degree of departure of the component configuration of an innovation from the earlier ones

Depending on the degree of departure being minor or excessive on the above-mentioned dimensions, the innovations can be classified into the following four categories:

- Incremental innovations
- Modular innovations
- Architectural innovations
- Radical innovations

These four types of innovations are being discussed as follows:

8.3.1 Incremental Innovations

These innovations involve minor departure from the earlier innovations, both in terms of specific technologies and component configuration. Most of the innovations (approximately 75 percent to 80 percent) fall in this category. These innovations can be planned by the business organizations as these require only minor change or alteration in the existing technologies and configuration. Continuous improvement efforts undertaken by the business organizations are a type of incremental innovations. Business organizations purposely use incremental innovations to introduce a stream of better products in the market one after the other. Incremental movement from Pentium I to Pentium IV is an example of exploiting the markets profitable by introducing one product after the other.

8.3.2 Modular Innovations

Modular innovations involve minor departure from the earlier innovations in terms of component configuration coupled with major departure from the earlier innovations, in terms of specific technologies. Movement from analogue to digital technology is an example of modular innovation. For bringing about modular innovations there is a pertinent need on the part of the organization to learn and acquire new technologies. Business organizations can usher in modular innovations by acquiring technologies from outside. Modular innovations are instrumental for creating wealth for the entrepreneur and the society, as the products based on earlier innovations are replaced by the products based on the new technologies. Replacement of telephone sets based on mechanical dialing to the ones based on push button dialing is an example in place.

8.3.3 Architectural Innovations

Architectural innovations involve the use of existing specific technologies for carving out the innovations by rearranging/reconfiguring of the components. As explained by the name, architectural innovations largely involve the change in the architecture of the product. Creation of mini versions of the products by introducing the architectural changes is an example of architectural innovations. Creation of portable TV sets and fans, refrigerators with the freezer at the bottom instead of top, etc. are the examples of architectural innovations. Technology integration is a good source of architectural innovations; whereby different existing technologies are put in a single product. Integration of mp3 player, camera, in a cell phone is an example of architectural innovation. Architectural innovations based on technology integration always carry a great economic potential for the business organizations.

8.3.4 Radical Innovations

A complete departure from the earlier innovations, both in terms of specific technologies and component configuration, represents radical innovation. These innovation although less frequent are the real contributors to the wealth of the society. Radical innovations are used to find out solutions to the problems where the extension of the existing technologies is not able to deliver the results. Radical innovations usually stem from the great leaps in the basic research, and are responsible for creation and demolition of the industries. Radical innovations are instrumental in extending the capabilities of the mankind. These innovations normally emerge from the public research agencies against other types of innovations that largely surface from the private domain. Success of Genome project and stem cell research can be termed as the radical innovations, as these innovations are going to create a new type of healthcare industry in the future, threatening the survival of the traditional pharmaceutical industry.

8.4 APPROPRIATION OF INTELLECTUAL PROPERTY

The process of appropriation of IP refers to the acquisition of IP by the organization. Primarily there are two ways of obtaining IP in the organizational setting, firstly, through in-house R&D, and secondly the acquisition through external sources or strategic alliances. In-house R&D is an important source of appropriation of IP. For the generation of potentially profitable IP, sound R&D management practices are must. Industrial R&D has evolved through a number of stages before reaching the present stage. Roussel et al. (1991) have classified the evolution of technology appropriation into three generations.

In first generation approach, future technologies of a company are decided largely by Research and Development managers with very little participation from general management personnel. This approach is characterized by absence of long-term strategic framework in context of R&D, treatment of R&D as an overhead cost and missing link between technology strategy and business strategy. Because of negligible communication between business managers and R&D managers, upward visibility of the technologies being developed is quite low. Technologies are created first and subsequently their use for business is thought upon. Overall, R&D works almost as a standalone unit in the organization and lacks in the linkages with the business.

Second generation approach to technology appropriation at the best can be defined as the transition stage between the first generation and the third generation. In the second generation approach, the interrelationship between various functional areas of management is recognized and efforts are made to increase communication between technology managers and business managers. This approach is characterized by the setting up of partial strategic framework, increased interaction between business and R&D although in form of sort of customer-supplier interaction and combined business/R&D insight at the project level.

In third generation approach to appropriation of technology, a conscious effort is made to create a strategically balanced portfolio of technology appropriation projects with joint efforts of both business managers and technology managers. Third generation approach to technology appropriation ensures both strategic and operational partnership among technology managers and business managers as against second generation approach that focuses only on operational partnership and omits strategic partnership. Third generation approach demolishes the isolation of R&D function and results in consistent business and R&D objectives.

Choice of technology appropriation projects should be based on a close linkage between technology strategy and corporate strategy so as to bring greatest value to the firm. Loss of linkage between technology strategy and corporate strategy may lead to value erosion. To avoid value erosion, it must be ensured that R&D function yields products and processes that serve the business needs of the firm well.

8.5 BEHAVIOURAL ASPECTS

In the emerging knowledge economy, the organizations are identifying creation of IP as an important business activity. In the process of creating IP, the source itself, i.e. human being cannot be ignored. Therefore, behavioural issues related to creation of IP become important. The following discussion deals with the issues such as creativity/innovation in the organization, role of leadership and the characteristics of innovative firms.

8.5.1 Creativity/Innovation

Business creativity leading to innovation is sum total of three components expertise, creative thinking skills and intrinsic motivation. According to intrinsic motivation principle of creativity, people will be most creative when they feel motivated primarily by the interest satisfaction and the challenges of the work itself and not by external pressure (Amabile, 1998). It is important to carve out an organizational culture that respects seemingly weird ideas and is tolerant towards failures. For fostering creativity in the organization right type of atmosphere, where new ideas can incubate, is an absolute necessity. For creating right type of atmosphere in the organization, managers should be able to match people with right assignments. It can be done by collecting and analyzing rich and detailed information about their employees and the available assignments. Knowledge workers should be provided autonomy concerning the means. Ends can be provided or pre-decided but how to do the job at hands should be left purely to the task performer. Managers normally are in a position to influence all the three components of business creativity. Most sensitive factor to managerial interventions from these factors is the motivation. It has been proven that this factor improves a lot even with a subtle positive change in the organization environment. Creativity is affected largely by the following factors in the organization (Amabile, 1998):

(a) by creating challenging atmosphere suitable for creativity
(b) by providing the required degree of freedom to knowledge workers
(c) by introducing team culture at workplace
(d) supporting creative endeavours with adequate resources
(e) relevant and apt management support

According to Drucker (2002) innovation can be sourced from unexpected occurrences, incongruities, process needs, market changes, demographic changes, perception changes and new knowledge. Innovation can be managed objectively and systematically if one is well equipped with the requisite skills. Initially computer was meant for advanced scientific work but suddenly if found applications in routine jobs such as payroll. Origin of systematic innovation lies at the heart of the analysis of the sources of new opportunities. As innovation can be both conceptual and perceptual both inductive and deductive methods of creating new knowledge can be successful. Effective innovations are often simple and well-focused. Greater the degree of obviousness, higher will be the effectiveness. As pure simplicity is the ultimate level of sophistication. Businesses should ensure that innovations involved in creating new users and new markets are directed toward a well-defined, clear and carefully designed application.

No substantial empirical evidence is available till date that innovative ability rests only with large firms. In a study of small firms Khan & Manopichetwattana (1989) have drawn several conclusions related to the innovative characteristics of these organizations. The characteristics of the first group, which the authors called "Young Turks", included being young and proactive having a strong research orientation, accepting risk taking and maintaining a focus on differentiation. The second group of innovators called "Blue Chips" was characterized by strong focus on management techniques such as environmental scanning and the integration of decision-making controls and analysis procedures.

8.5.2 Characteristics of Innovating Organizations

Degree of innovation of an organization is determined by a number of factors. The following characteristics are commonly found in the organizations with higher degree of innovation:

- Open Atmosphere
- Tolerance for Failure
- Free Communication
- Quest for Knowledge
- Decentralization
- Management Support

These characteristics are being discussed in brief as follows:

Open Atmosphere

Innovation is directly affected by the degree of formalization in the organization. Innovations can be nurtured under an open atmosphere with negligible bureaucratic obstacles. Higher degree of bureaucracy dampens the spirit of innovation in the organization. Therefore, the organizations with less formalization can be expected to be more innovative.

Tolerance for Failure

Not all the efforts for garnering innovation meet with success and fear of punishment in case of failure may undermine the promptness of the employees to share new ideas and undertake innovative projects. Therefore, tolerance for failures acts as a stimulant for the innovative activities within the organization. Innovative organizations usually have good appraisals in place and tolerate the failures that may come in pursuit of doing something different.

Free Communication

Innovative organizations always communicate freely both within as well as outside the organization. Informal communication leads to better social ties and expand the horizon of innovation opportunities beyond the boundaries of the organization. Cross-functional interaction within the organization arising out of free and informal communication throws open the window for creating cross disciplinary ideas and knowledge.

Quest for Knowledge

Innovative organizations value new ideas and knowledge. Therefore, these organizations have a very strong quest for knowledge. Innovative organizations are always open to creating partnerships for having access to new and superior knowledge.

Decentralization

Decentralized decision-making is very helpful in promoting new ideas and innovations. Decentralization empowers the employee to lower down the organizational chart and unleashes the power of innovative minds across the board.

Management Support

Support from top management is also an important dimension affecting innovating capabilities of an organization. By ensuring adequate resource allocation to the projects and assuming overall responsibility for providing conducive atmosphere for innovating endeavours, management support can certainly make a difference to the innovating character of the firm. Innovative organizations invariably have strong support from the management.

8.6 SUMMARY

Intellectual property acts as a source for generating wealth for the entrepreneur in particular and for society in general. Intellectual property is important for business as it increases the revenue and creates entry barriers for the potential rivals. Business may require intellectual property for altering the industry architecture and supporting the existing IP. Process of creation of IP starts with the tacit ideas generated by the human thought process. These ideas are codified and validated through the process of experimentation. Explicit scientific and business knowledge passes through internal and external scrutiny before getting converted to intellectual property. Based on the departure from the earlier innovation on the basis of specific technologies and configuration, the innovations can be categorized in four categories, namely, incremental innovations, modular innovations, architectural innovations and radical innovations. Technology appropriation has moved from first generation to the third generation leading to synchronization between R&D managers and business managers. Organizational culture and leadership play an important role in the creation of IP. Innovating organizations usually have free and open atmosphere for germination of ideas into innovations that can be exploited profitably.

CASE STUDY—HARNESSING INNOVATION AND INTELLECTUAL PROPERTY AT TATA

The name Tata has been respected in India for 140 years for its adherence to strong values and business ethics. Tata group in India is one of the world's largest conglomerates with presence in every major international market. Tata companies operate in seven business sectors—communications and information technology, engineering, materials, services, energy, consumer products and chemicals. The total revenue of Tata companies, taken together, was $ 70.8 billion (around ₹325,334 crore) in 2008–2009. Out of this total, about 64.7 percent share comes from business outside India, with total employee strength of around 357,000 people worldwide.

INTELLECTUAL PROPERTY—A PRIORITY

Like so many other business groups Tata has been able to identify the potential of IP for the future business and competitive landscape. Tata group has learnt the importance of IP in its own way, ranging from the instance of Tata Steel not getting protected the breakthrough innovation in the steel making process (the coal based direct reduction of iron) in the 1970s to owning of bounty of 850 patents, copyrights and applications. This change in Tata group has been the result of the conscious effort of top management for reorienting the group vision by assigning due importance to IP. Seeking excellence in innovation the group articulates:

"Innovation—in thoughts, processes, approaches and strategies—has become a critical factor for Tata companies as they chart course for a future in a business world without boundaries. The objective is to consistently deliver breakthrough products and services and Tata sees innovation as the means to achieve this."

For achieving the excellence in innovation Tata started a number of initiatives and two important initiatives in this regard are being presented as follows:

Tata Group Innovation Forum (TGIF)

TGIF is managed by Tata Quality Management Services and is involved in organizing a number of workshops and events to facilitate interaction among Tata companies for stimulating innovative thinking. The major activities of TGIF have been summarized as follows:

1. ***Innovation Workshops:*** TGIF organizes workshops and seminars by inviting the experts and academicians for introducing new innovation concepts to Tata managers.
2. ***Thought Leadership through Publications:*** Tata Management Training Centre at Pune comes out with publications featuring articles and case studies on innovation.
3. ***Innovation Awards:*** Celebration of 'Tata Innovation Day' to recognize innovators in the Tata group.

4. ***Technology and Research Clusters:*** For creating the opportunities for technological innovation, TGIF brings together technologists and researchers from different Tata companies.

Tata IP Program (TIPP)

TIPP has been recently launched to give a push to reinvent innovation in Tata group. Under TIPP, IP clusters have been created at Bangalore, Pune and Jamshedpur. Under TIPC, the flagship companies (Tata Steel at Jamshedpur, Tata Motors at Pune, Titan Industries, Tata Tea and TCS at Bangalore) are expected to mentor associates in innovations and technological advances. This exercise is aimed at identifying; creating, protecting and leveraging IP assets for building a quality portfolio that cam provide a competitive advantage and open up new business opportunities. Taking clue from the recently acquired foreign businesses, an attempt is being made to come up with a closely knitted IP system.

ISSUES FOR DISCUSSION

1. Tata has a number of companies dealing in different businesses. Discuss the relevance and efficacy of TGIF for diverse businesses at Tata. Can there be an alternative to TGIF for harnessing innovations at Tata?
2. Discuss the pros and cons of TIPP in context of generating more IP at Tata.
3. What else can be done for harnessing innovations and IP at Tata?

Discussion Questions

1. Why there is a need to create intellectual property in business?
2. Discuss in detail the process of creation of knowledge/IP.
3. Elaborate the characteristics of the innovating organizations.
4. Citing suitable examples, discuss in detail various types of innovations.
5. What are the important behavioural considerations for creation of IP?
6. Differentiate between 'Modular Innovations' and 'architectural Innovations'.
7. Write short note on the following:
   (a) Business Creativity
   (b) Third generation approach to appropriation of technology
   (c) Use of IP as entry barrier
8. "Level of creativity in an organization can be managed". Comment on the statement.

Objective Type Questions

Tick the right answer in given multiple-choice questions:

1. Intellectual property can be used for
   (a) Enacting entry barriers (b) Increasing revenue
   (c) Entering new markets (d) All of these
2. The process by which tacit knowledge is communicated to others is called:
   (a) Validation (b) Codification (c) Experimentation
   (d) None of these
3. An innovation with minor departure from earlier innovations in terms of specific technologies and major departure in terms of configuration is termed as
   (a) Incremental (b) Radical (c) Modular (d) Architectural
4. An innovation with major departure from earlier innovations in terms of specific technologies and minor departure in terms of configuration is termed as
   (a) Incremental (b) Radical (c) Modular (d) Architectural
5. An innovation with minor departure from earlier innovations in terms of specific technologies as well as in terms of configuration is termed as
   (a) Incremental (b) Radical (c) Modular (d) Architectural
6. An innovation with major departure from earlier innovations in terms of specific technologies as well as in terms of configuration is termed as
   (a) Incremental (b) Radical (c) Modular (d) Architectural
7. R&D is treated as an overhead cost in which generation of appropriability of technology
   (a) First (b) Second (c) Third (d) None of these
8. Which of the following factors is not expected to increase innovative capability of an organization:
   (a) Lesser formalization (b) Management support
   (c) Decentralization (d) Openness
9. Out of the following which type of innovation is most prevalent
   (a) Incremental (b) Radical (c) Modular (d) Architectural
10. An innovation with major departure from earlier innovations in terms of specific technologies as well as in terms of configuration is termed as
    (a) Incremental (b) Radical (c) Modular (d) Architectural

Mark TRUE or FALSE against given statements:

1. Radical innovation occur quite frequently. (True/False)
2. Any scientific knowledge can be converted to IP. (True/False)

3. Lesser formalization promotes innovation in the organization. (True/False)
4. Centralization discourages innovation in the organization. (True/False)
5. IP can be used as an entry barrier. (True/False)

References

Amabile, T.M. (1998), How to kill creativity. September, *Harvard Business Review*.

Drucker, P.F. (2002), Discipline of innovation. August, *Harvard Business Review*.

Henderson, R.M. and Clark, K.B. (1990), Architectural innovations: The reconfiguration of existing technologies and failure of established firms. *Administrative Science Quarterly*, Volume 35, pp. 9–30.

Khan, A.M. and Manopicherwattana, V. (1989), Innovative and non-innovative small firms: types and Characteristics, *Management Science*, Volume 35, No. 5, pp. 597–606.

Roussel, P.O., Saad, K.M. and Erickson, T.J.C. (1991), *Third Generation R&D*, Cambridge, MA, *Harvard Business School Press*.

CHAPTER 9

Intellectual Property Management

Knowledge management and new product creation are expected to become the major determinants of competitive advantage available to knowing organization in the emerging knowledge economies. The world is witnessing a shift in the determinants of development from manufacturing to service sector and from capital resources to knowledge resources. In the emerging knowledge economy worldwide the paradigms are shifting from physical to knowledge resources. Nature of the businesses is undergoing change on this count as increasingly the businesses are turning from being capital-intensive to knowledge-intensive. For dealing with this type of emerging situation, there is an urgent need for changing the focus of the business planning and management. Intellectual property differs from the physical property in a number of ways; therefore, the methods of managing physical property in the traditional business cannot be extended to the domain of intellectual property. According to the available estimates, by late 1990s approximately 75 percent of market capitalization of the Fortune 100 companies was accounted for by intellectual property assets, such as patents, copyrights and trade marks. Another estimate by the economists at Brookings Institution suggests a marked shift from physical assets to knowledge assets. According to this estimate, physical asset such as plant and machinery, equipment, etc., were accounting for 62 percent of market value in case of manufacturing companies and this contribution has reduced to 30 percent by the start of this millennium. First decade of twenty first century has witnessed an increase in the filing of IP applications and this trend is expected to catch up further. In light of these facts IP management requires due attention in a business organization and cannot be left only to technology managers. There is pertinent need to have IP management in place so that maximum value can be derived from IP and knowledge assets.

9.1 DEFINING IP MANAGEMENT

Management of acquisition, exploitation, and protection of intellectual property of an organization, for the purpose of capturing maximum value currently and ensuring the sustainability of IP assets for the future, can be termed as IP management. IP management seeks to derive competitive advantage for the organization by coordinating the entire IP value chain of the organization ranging from IP creation to IP enforcement. IP management is assuming more importance as market value of the firms is increasingly being determined by IP and knowledge assets.

9.2 NEED AND IMPORTANCE OF IP MANAGEMENT

IP management is relatively a new addition to the field in management, and has started acquiring strategic importance in the organizational settings. Need and importance of IP management is growing day-by-day on account of the following reasons:

1. Share of IP and knowledge assets in the firm valuation is increasing and these assets deserve to have adequate attention.
2. IP management can be crucial for the survival of an organization in the emerging knowledge economy.
3. Value derived from IP may be undermined in the absence of proper IP management.
4. Sound IP management is the pre-requisite for the sustenance of IP ecosystem in the organization.
5. Value originating from IP of an organization may be captured by other organization if safeguards through good IP management are not put in place.
6. Superior IP management can benefit the customers, in particular and society, in general through improved product and services.

Reitzig (2007) has tried to explore the relationship between IP strategy and performance. The results from the study indicated that the alignment between intellectual property and business strategy has become sophisticated, and is cause for differentiated performance. Further, for dealing with IP-based competition, management attention is required at all levels, i.e., functional, business unit and corporate. Moreover, informal information exchange between the key persons leads to better performance.

9.3 MAJOR IP MANAGEMENT ACTIVITIES

IP management involves a number of functions and activities. The major IP management activities in the organizational settings are being listed and explained briefly as follows:

1. **Undertaking IP Intelligence** which deals with the understanding of the current and potential changes in the IP landscape that can be

crucial to the performance and status of the organization in time to come. Both macro and micro level changes are considered while gathering IP intelligence.

2. **Acquisition of IP** involves acquiring IP for venturing into new businesses as well as supporting the existing ones, both through internal and external sources. Acquisition of IP is considered as the prime function of IP management.
3. **While Managing or deciding about IP Portfolio**, the composition of IP portfolio is also an important activity of IP management. This activity deals with the decision of strengthening and pruning of IP assets in the IP portfolio.
4. **Supporting Deployment IP in products and services** deals with supporting the embedding of the available IP in products and services and deals with the development of new products and services. Role of IP management also becomes important in light of the possibility of infringing IP of others during the new product development process.
5. **Commercialization of IP** deals with translating the existing IP assets into real monetary gains. As poor commercialization can give away the advantage available from IP, this activity is considered as the most important IP management activity.
6. **Protecting IP management** also involves protecting the organizational IP assets from the external infringements and market moves by the competitors by taking suitable and timely actions.
7. **Putting IP Policy in place** also deals with the preparation and implementation of IP policy in the organization so that employees and other stakeholders are able to understand in IP management practices and procedures.
8. **Carrying out IP Audits** is also involved in the activity of carrying out IP audits so that organizational IP can be exploited optimally and least opportunities of benefitting from IP are lost.

For successful management of IP in the organization it is important to have synergy among the various IP management activities. For better understanding of various IP management activities listed above a detailed discussion is being presented in the following section.

9.3.1 Undertaking IP Intelligence

As IP has assumed strategic importance in the business settings, it becomes important to be ready for the future time period. IP intelligence involves bringing out description of the existing IP landscape, identifying the trends that are expected to usher in potential changes in future and alternative descriptions of future changes. IP intelligence is the process of understanding the existing

IP scenario as well as the likely future scenario that is expected to affect the organization's business activities. IP intelligence acts as an input for the strategic decision makers and its accuracy affects the quality of strategic decisions made by the top management. IP intelligence also provides new insights to the organization by introducing of macro and micro level changes taking place in the outer world. These new insights can be instrumental in fostering the innovation and IP creation streams in the organization. IP intelligence is both external and internal in nature. Internal IP intelligence is able to describe the existing as well as potential IP landscape within the organization.

Environmental mapping can be undertaken for garnering IP intelligence. The process of environmental mapping consists of the following steps:

- Scanning
- Monitoring
- Forecasting
- Assessing

1. ***Scanning:*** Environmental scanning is performed to identify the signals and indicators of a significant innovation or technology change. Purpose of the scanning is to alert the organization about the potential changes that are likely to impact its business activities. Scanning is able to provide information on the potential problems that are to be tackled as well as the opportunities that can be exploited to the benefit of organization.
2. ***Monitoring:*** Trends and the events identified during the scanning process are monitored over a period of time. Monitoring basically involves tracking the technology changes over time. Patterns detected from the monitoring process can be helpful in getting ready for the future events such as creation of potential competitive IP and technology.
3. ***Forecasting:*** Forecasting involves the process of carving out the possible evolutionary curves of innovations and technologies monitored during the previous step. Forecasting provides important data to the organization regarding the scope, intensity and speed with which new technologies are evolving. Forecasting evolution speed of the technologies that are closely related to the organization helps in assigning priority to the counter measures. There are a number of techniques that can be used forecasting technologies and innovations, few of these have been listed as follows:
    - Scenario based forecasting
    - S-curve approach
    - Simulation
    - Delphi technique
    - Morphological analysis

4. ***Assessing:*** Process of assessing involves finding out how likely the changes are going to affect the organization and evaluation of the organization in context of these likely changes. Possible response options to the future events are also identified at this stage keeping in view the capabilities of the organization and the severity of the likely changes.

9.3.2 Acquisition of IP

Organizations acquire IP for entering new markets, protecting the existing IP and products and increasing revenue. Primarily, there are two sources for acquiring IP, i.e., inhouse R&D and external sourcing of IP. Creation and acquisition of IP from inhouse R&D has been discussed in Chapter 8. External sources are also a good option for acquisition of IP. One way of acquiring IP is 'Licensing in', whereby an organization can license IP from the other organizations. Major sources of licensing-in of IP have been listed as follows:

- Other companies
- Universities and educational institutions
- Government research agencies

Major external sources of IP in India include Center for Scientific and Industrial Research (CSIR), Defense Research and Development Organization (DRDO), Indian Institutes of Technology (IITs) and Universities.

Apart from licensing in, organizations can use the external sources for acquisition of IP in the following manner:

- Participation in research consortiums
- Entering into strategic alliances

Participation in Research Consortiums

In face of stiff global competition, rapid technological changes and inflating research budgets many organizations prefer to go for cooperative research and development. By making research consortiums, the organizations are able to work on technology platforms that crucial for enhancing the competitiveness of the industry as a whole. This sort of joint effort not only benefits the participating organizations through additions in their IP portfolios but is also helpful in cutting down the wasteful expenditure that may be resulting because of duplication of the research effort in the absence of cooperation. Trade associations and industry associations are normally the driving forces behind establishing research consortiums.

Entering into Strategic Alliances

Organizations may join hands with other organizations for creation of technology and IP. This type of joint effort differs from research consortiums on the ground that the number of participating organizations on case of strategic alliance is quite limited, at times restricted to two to three organizations. For the purpose of acquisition of IP strategic alliances may surface in two forms namely, collaboration/joint venture and corporate venturing. Collaboration means two or more organizations coming together for a limited period of time for creation and exploitation of IP. If two or more organizations float a separate organization for this purpose, then this arrangement is called joint venture. Another popular form of IP acquisition practice is called corporate venturing. Under corporate venturing, a large firm established a relationship with a smaller firm by providing capital and distribution/marketing expertise. Larger firm benefits from the acquisition of IP and smaller firms are able to have access to capital and distribution/marketing expertise.

Making a choice between internal and external sources of IP acquisition is an important decision. This decision depends on the extent of need of IP and the capability of the organization to appropriate IP inhouse. If a firm feels that a given IP is strategically important to it, but inhouse R&D capabilities are not good enough for acquiring IP, then external sources are preferred. In case the strong inhouse R&D is there, IP acquisition is attempted internally.

9.3.3 Managing IP Portfolio

IP portfolio carries a maintenance cost inform of fees paid on account of renewal and cost of efforts made for protecting it from external infringements. An attempt should be made to strengthen the existing IP portfolio by means of acquiring new IP that can prevent 'inventing around' attempts of the competitors with respect to the existing IP. With passage of time, a few IP assets may start losing their revenue earning capabilities. For such type of IP assets 'licensing out' attempt should be made. IP assets that are not adding any value to the revenue streams should be pruned out and discontinued for further renewals. Similarly, depending on the opportunities, the possibility of cross-licensing can also be explored.

9.3.4 Supporting Deploying IP in Products and Services

If capabilities and resources are available then the firm may like to deploy IP in the products and services for making commercial gains in the market place. Translating the available IP assets into products and services is an important IP management activity. In the fast-paced business environment, time to market becomes an important factor for garnering first mover advantages as well as extension of time window for commercially exploiting the product in the marketplace. Sound IP management can be instrumental in decreasing time to market by active participation of IP managers in the new product development process. By employing techniques such as concurrent engineering, the firms can reduce time for new product development. Participation of IP managers at the conceptual stage of product development not only provides sufficient time for acquiring IP from the external sources (if required) but also provides more product development options through the possibility of combining internal IP with potential IP acquisitions from the external sources.

Still another benefit of involving IP managers early in the new product development process is the enhanced capability of detecting potential infringement by the organization on IP of other organizations. Participation of IP managers can ensure early abandonment of new product development, if any such infringement is taking place. Early abandonment in such cases can save the cost and resources for the organization and can also help avoiding walking into legal conflict later on. There are a number of organizations, termed as 'Patent Sharks', that take benefit of other organizations inadvertently infringing upon their IP and claim hefty damages afterwards. A brief discussion on patent sharks has been presented in Chapter 10.

9.3.5 Commercialization of IP

Commercialization of IP is the process of translating IP assets into monetary gains. Commercialization of IP is usually carried out by converting it into products and services by the organization itself and licensing out IP to others for earning royalties. Acquisition of IP involves substantial investment and an organization's innovation system cannot be run by fuelling in fresh investments perpetually. For sustainability of R&D function in an organization, commercialization of IP becomes must as the cash inflows arising from the present IP assets can be used for funding the creation and acquisition of more IP assets in the future.

If an organization is having adequate resources, skill and opportunities in place, it can go on converting IP assets into products and undertake manufacturing, distribution and marketing activities for earning revenues. But for some reasons, if the organization is not interested in undertaking the activities mentioned above, then revenue stream from IP assets can be used by means of licensing. A license is an agreement between a firm that owns IP (the licensor) and a firm (licensee) that is willing to pay a lump sum amount or a certain amount of royalties in order to manufacture, use and sell products that incorporated the IP. Licensing out means assigning license of own IP to other firm for a consideration and licensing in means paying royalties to the other firm to gets license of its IP. Decision to license in or license out depends on the capabilities of the organization in the end product market. Normally, the following two methods are used for commercialization of IP:

- Licensing Out
- Cross-Licensing

Economic rationale behind these options is being discussed briefly as follows:

Licensing Out

Licensing out is basically a decision based on the trade-off between the revenue gained through receipt of royalties and the loss of sales revenue due to increased competition in the market. In other words, if an organization decides against licensing out, it can benefit from being the lone seller in the market place, but it will not have any income from the royalties. On the other hand, by licensing out IP an organization is creating competition in the market place for itself leading to decrease in the sales revenue but revenue from licensing in form of royalties will start to flow in. At times smaller organizations not being in position to undertake manufacturing, distribution and marketing activities prefer to license out their IP.

Cross-Licensing

Organizations in certain industries, such as computers and semiconductors go for cross-licensing their patents to one another. Due to overlapping of the technology in these industries, prime motive of cross-licensing is to avoid endless infighting and litigation.

Lichtenthaler (2007) has tried to identify the reasons for licensing of IP apart from revenue generation and gaining reciprocity in accessing IP of others' (cross-licensing). These reasons have been listed as follows:

- To consciously find adopters for establishing own IP as the industry standard
- To identify intended or unintended infringement of IP so that profit may be generated from infringements
- To increase the speed of firm's R&D operations through feedback and learning effects
- To get freedom to operate by means of cross-licensing

For superior commercialization of IP and technology, Nevens, et al. (1990) state that companies should measure and improve their commercialization capability. Important dimensions determining the capability of a company to commercialize include time to market, range of markets, number of products, and breadth of technology. Further, companies can build their commercialization capability by making commercialization top priority of the top management, setting goal and benchmarks for commercialization, developing cross-functional skills among employees and directly involving managers to expedite actions and decisions pertaining to commercialization.

1. ***Licensing Agreement:*** Licensing is an agreement between the licensor and the licensee. Enforceable by the law, a licensing

agreement becomes a contract, and is legally binding on the licensor as well as the licensee. Major heads of a licensing agreement are being listed as follows:

(i) *Parties:* This part of the licensing agreement contains the description of the licensor and the licensee along with their addresses.

(ii) *Subject matter and territory:* This part of the licensing agreement deals with matters, such as exclusivity (whether the licensor is free to license to other parties), field of use (markets and geographical territories), duration (the term of the licensing agreement), sublicensing (whether the licensee can use sub-license the IP to other parties) and modification (who owns the improvement made by the licensee).

(iii) *Licensor's obligations:* This part deals with the general obligations and responsibilities of the licensor.

(iv) *Licensee's obligations:* This part deals with the general obligations and responsibilities of the licensee.

(v) *Financial consideration:* This part includes the royalty structure (the manner of calculating royalty, such as percentage of sales revenue, royalty based on number of product sold), annual minimum royalty and upfront payment.

Important Considerations for Licensing

Licensing can be seen as a mechanism to exploit IP available with the firm in monetary consideration. Licensing process has got a number of facets including monetary stakes, legal and strategic dimensions. For effective management of IP in the organization, it becomes vital to consider all the aspects of licensing, because the mistakes made at this stage of IP management may prove to be irreparable. There are number of dimensions deserving attention before entering into licensing contract and these dimensions are crucial for both the parties, i.e., licensor as well as licensee. Important considerations at the time of licensing are being listed as follows:

- Exclusivity
- Territory
- Revocability
- Field of Use

These considerations are being discussed in the following section.

1. ***Exclusivity:*** At the time of licensing out an IP or a technology (with IP embedded in it), it is important to specify whether the licensing is exclusive or not. Exclusivity is an important dimension in the licensing contract. An 'Exclusive License' ensures that no other

party than the licensee is having a right to use the IP or technology. An exclusive license mounts to even the exclusion of the licensor from the right of using the IP or technology. On the other hand, if the licensor reserves the right to use IP/technology, but excludes all other parties but the licensee, the license is termed as a sole license. An exclusive license ensures that the licensee becomes a virtual owner of IP or technology subject to the conditions laid in the licensing contract. It is worth mentioning that the licensor has number of ways to deal with the exclusivity. A license may be restricted in exclusivity in terms of time period, territory and the field of use. Employment of a specific way or the combinations depends on the nature of IP or technology. In practice, exclusive licenses and sole licenses are not granted broadly on account of two major reasons. Firstly, these situations limit the ability of the licensor to exploit the value of IP or technology fully and secondly, anti-monopoly or competition regulations discourage these types of licensing.

2. ***Territory:*** At the time of grant of IP to an organization, the law of the land provides the territorial rights, i.e., the rights of the owner are restricted to the borders of that country. For example, patent in India is a territorial right and as such does not extend beyond the borders of the country. At the same time international treaties and conventions provide for the systems that ensure that these rights can be extended to the foreign lands subject to the fulfillment of certain requirements and procedures. Depending on the jurisdiction of the IP right and the nature of IP or technology, it should be explicitly mentioned in the license contract that whether the license is limited to the territory of the home country or extends to other foreign countries. In case the rights are available, to the licensor, even in the foreign countries, the names of such territories should be clearly mentioned in the licensing contract. Territory is an important consideration both at the time of acquisition of IP (applying for grant of IP) as well as licensing IP.
3. ***Revocability:*** It is important for the licensee to ensure that license contract contains an irrevocability clause. In absence of this clause, the licensor has the right to cancel the license at any time. Inclusion of the irrevocability clause guarantees that the licensor is not in a position to cancel the license, unless there is a breach of contract by the licensee leading to the cancellation. In event of the revocation of a bare license, the licensee cannot claim any damages from the licensor. It becomes difficult for the licensor to revoke a contractual license as the licensee is in a position to claim damages from the licensor as per the specifications of the contract.
4. ***Field of use:*** Depending on the nature of the IP, scope of the rights associated with the IP may vary. It is purely a deal between

the contracting parties to restrict the scope of the rights while undertaking the licensing process. License contract may provide that the licensee will use the IP or technology only for a specific purpose or a specific industrial application. On account of convergence of the technologies, it becomes important to mention the field of use in the license contract. It is quite possible that initially an IP or technology is viewed to have limited use, but subsequently on account of external changes there is an enlargement in the scope of IP or technology use. It is strongly recommended that the field of use should be clearly mentioned in the license contract. The language of the license contract should be put through expert scrutiny so as to avoid a situation where the license contract provides the rights to the licensee far beyond the anticipation of the licensor. This is especially valid for the fields, such as chemistry, biotechnology and materials.

Apart from the above consideration, the licensor should explicitly mention that the IP or technology is 'non-transferable', because omission of the term may enable the licensee to transfer rights to the third party even without the permission of the licensor, unless specified so in the contract. Further, the mechanism and procedure related to sub-licensing should preferably be explicitly dealt with in the licensing contract.

Valuation of Intellectual Property

Intellectual Property is an intangible asset. Therefore, the problems faced in the valuation of intangible assets are applicable for IP as well. Nevertheless, the valuation of IP of the organization is important from the perspective of making effective R&D decisions as well as maximizing the exploits available from IP. Valuation of IP is not anyone's job, hence, in case of non-availability of the requisite skills in-house, hiring the services of the external experts is highly recommended. Apart from deciding the royalty from licensing the IP or technology, valuation of IP plays an important role during the sale, mergers and acquisitions of the business which the IP is part of.

Mainly three approaches to valuation of IP are available and listed as follows:

- Cost-based Approach
- Income-based Approach
- Market-based Approach

These approaches are being discussed as follows:

1. ***Cost-based approach:*** Considered as the simple and basic approach to valuation of IP, cost-based approach makes an attempt to value IP on the basis of the cost that has been accrued in creating/acquiring IP. Getting information on all aspects of cost related to generation of IP is an uphill task itself and getting this information correctly is still a

bigger challenge. Cost-based approach is considered suitable for the situation where the organization is looking for a target rate of return from IP. At the same time, this approach suffers from the limitation on account of historical cost information available from the books of accounts.

2. ***Income-based approach:*** Income-based approach seeks to determine the value of IP on the basis of the income likely to be available in future. Valuation process under this approach decides the value of IP as the sum total of all the future income streams adjusted to the present value. Income-based approach to valuation of IP is considered superior to the cost-based approach, but suffers from the limitations associated the projections and forecasts. Needless to say, the efficiency of valuation through this method depends on the accuracy of projections made by the experts.
3. ***Market-based approach:*** This approach aims to find out the valuation of similar IP or technology available in the market and determines the value of the IP under question accordingly. If market information sought under this approach is available, the valuation of IP is considered as the most accurate and reliable as compared to the above-mentioned approaches of valuation. Even if market information needed for the valuation is not available, valuation of an IP can be determined through the auction. It is worth mentioning that in absence of the required market information, deciding the reserve price becomes a nagging issue.

Decision regarding the choice of the approach is guided by the nature of IP under consideration as well as the policy of the organization. It may be good idea to follow more than one approach to deal with the complexities involved in the valuation of IP.

9.3.6 Protecting IP

IP acquisitions involve huge investment and are the sources for revenue generation for the organization. Therefore, conscious efforts are required to protect IP from being lost or getting devalued. The mechanisms which IP assets can lose their value are being listed as follows:

- Inventing around
- Infringement
- Obsolescence

These mechanisms are being discussed as follows:

1. ***Inventing around:*** It is the process by which competitors, suppliers or customers are able to acquire IP by maneuvering around IP assets of the organization. On account of this inventing around, value of

IP decreases considerably and expected revenue streams from the IP asset may start drying down.

2. ***Infringement:*** It is the situation where a competitor or other party manufactures, uses, markets products based on IP of an organization without its consent or license. Although being illegal, infringements can substantially lower the potential value of an IP asset.
3. ***Obsolescence:*** Competitors may create an IP which is superior to the IP of the organization. If newly created IP is superior by quite a distance, it may well lead to making the preexisting IP obsolete.

For protecting the value of IP, an organization can use two options. Firstly, it can seek legal remedies against the infringing parties, hence, discouraging future infringements. Secondly, it can invest in complementary assets such as strong manufacturing and distribution network that can ward off attempts of inventing around and rendering IP assets obsolete. For getting sustainable protection in the market place, the companies may use combination of different types of IP such as combining a patent with trade mark. As patents are protected for a limited time period efforts are required for bundling them with new IP so that IP can be exploited even after it comes into public domain. Trade marks can be protected endlessly; therefore, it is highly advisable to combine trade marks and patents. Once established in the market place, trade marks can be helpful in generating benefits from otherwise phased out products.

9.3.7 Putting IP Policy in Place

For promoting the involvement of the individuals in creation of IP, IP policy can play a major role. An IP policy is basically a set of guidelines that deals with the issues such as ownership, protection, commercialization and benefit sharing with respect to IP created in an organization. IP policy contains employee covenants, i.e., contract between the employee and the employer for protection of employer's intellectual property. In this respect, IP policy usually contains the assignment clause, non-competing clause, confidentiality clause. Assignment is the process of assigning ownership of IP created during the job stint, non-competing clause deals with forbidding a former employee directly competing with the employer for a specific time period and confidentiality clause deals with the requirement on part of the employee to maintain secrecy and use the information for the benefit of the employer. IP policy also helps the organization to choose among the competing claims within the organization for the purpose of filing application to seek award of IP. There can be many claims coming up in an organization with the potential being converted into IP asset. IP policy guides the selection among the candidate opportunities for further taking up the process of applying for registration and seeking legal protection. Further, if the process of deciding about the ownership, commercialization and benefit is clear and transparent, then researchers working in the private as well as public sector feel more motivated to create IP. IP policy lays down the detailed procedure of acquiring IP based on the research work being carried out in the organization, the support and facilitation available for commercialization and sharing of the ownership and benefits between researchers and the organization. IP policy becomes more relevant in context of educational institutes, universities and public research agencies as the employees can clearly see and share the fruits available from their hard work and knowledge efforts.

9.3.8 Carrying Out IP Audits

An IP audit is the process of making an assessment of the IP assets of an organization. This process helps the organization to approximate the value of IP assets quantitatively. IP audit also helps to identify the strengths and weaknesses in the processes starting from the research stage to commercialization and protection of IP assets in the organization. Report of IP audit can help in improving the processes used in managing IP, hence, adding value to the firm. IP assets have already started figuring prominently during the valuation of a firm, and this trend is likely to further pick up in the future. IP audits provide useful information at the time of selling or acquiring a company. Apart from this, useful information on infringements, ownership rights related to third party and suggestions for strengthening specific IP assets in the future can be availed from IP audits.

9.4 5Cs MODEL OF MANAGING IP

For managing intellectual property at the firm level, managers should focus on the 5Cs namely carving, creating, commercializing, capturing and conserving. Carving the intellectual property right policy at the organizational level and aligning it with the organizational strategy is the first task in managing intellectual property. Creating intellectual property in the organization in a time phased manner by selecting a right balance of incremental and radical innovations is also important ingredient in effective intellectual property management. Commercializing the intellectual property portfolio of the organization is the most vital function of intellectual property management. Capturing involves deriving maximum out of the potential benefits available through commercialization through the use of complementary assets. Final activity related to intellectual property management is conserving the intellectual property of the enterprise from external infringements. These activities are being discussed in the following section.

9.4.1 Carving

First and the foremost, Intellectual Property (IP) related activity in the organization is carving out an IPR policy that is well-aligned with the strategy of the firm. For accomplishing the activity, there is a pertinent need on the part of the top leaders in the organization to identify the importance of IP as a key resource for the organization. Lot many times, mission statements of the companies may miss recognition of IP. Sound IP planning involves carving out an IPR policy and organizational structure for managing IP. As IP management is an organization-wide activity, it should not be left only to the selected departments, such as research and new product development. Increasingly companies are throwing up designations, such as CTO, CKO, etc. It is highly desirable that such designations and designated persons come out of paper and mark their impact in the real business working.

9.4.2 Creating

Creating basically deals with the process of technology appropriation in the organization. At the end of this activity, IP in the organization is available for exploitation in terms of monetary gains. Human imagination as a result of deep-rooted combinations of subconscious propels abundant and novel ideas in plenty. Sound IP management advocates for a planned and structured system that can multiply ideas, information and knowledge spread across the dimensions of the organization. Present state-of-the-art in almost every domain has reached a stage where solo technology expeditions are no longer capable of yielding actionable results. Therefore, there is an obvious need to combine the existing as well as new thinking across the multiple disciplines to come up with products and processes that are credible enough to provide landscape for incubation of new solutions. For accomplishing the activity of capturing a mechanism is required that is focused both within and outside the organization. Companies need to have a Knowledge Management System that captures information related to potential technology advances and latest customer needs. Further, potential technology advances and emerging customer needs should be combined to look for possible technology trajectories. Formality and bureaucratic curbs act as a dampener to the informal knowledge management process. Therefore, Knowledge Management System, in place, should ensure that free and informal interaction is allowed across different disciplines of technology so that fruitful combinations can be identified and exploited without wasting any time. For hastening up the successful completion of products based on multiple technology advances, complementary technologies existing in form of IP should be accessed or licensed in, without any hesitation. Managing capturing activity well by ensuring integration across the enterprise and industry cannot only result in benefits at enterprise level but also have enormous benefits for the society and customers. Integration avoids duplication and promotes borrowing complementary IP leading to benefits for all the stakeholders.

9.4.3 Commercializing

Creating IP is not enough, it is important to realize the commercial benefits from

IP-based assets. Commercialization of IP should be taken as the most important activity in IP management. Commercialization process ensures cash inflows for the organization and promotes future IP creation activity. Newly created technologies are to be embedded in products and services that create value for the customers. Although, a part of IP portfolio may be used for creating entry barriers but most of the IP assets are instrumental in generating direct benefits in terms of cash inflows. For exploiting the benefits from IP it is important that these are treated as assets that can be sold and purchased. It has been seen that organizations are able to create IP and get it protected, but subsequently find it very difficult to commercialize. Once protected IP is in place only then efforts are started for finding ways and means for earning money from these assets. To avoid creating IP that carries little value for commercialization, it is advisable to follow concurrent engineering approach, and involve the business managers from the beginning of the project.

9.4.4 Capturing

Pisano and Teece (2007) have argued that along with creating value through innovation it is also important to capture that value. There is a possibility of value of IP being siphoned off by the other parties such as the suppliers, customers and the competitors. For economic benefit of both the innovator and the society, insufficient capture of IP value is not desirable. IP environment and the industry architecture are the important determinants of value capture from IP. Further, for exploiting maximum value from IP complementary products, technologies and services are also required. Bhatia and Carey (2007) have emphasized that it is possible to make more money with fewer patents by focusing on securing only the essential protections that are required for exploiting the innovation. Companies deriving higher-than-average profitability from their IP assets were found to share the following characteristics—a strong market focus, a holistic view and stress on building strong organizational structure supporting IP.

9.4.5 Conserving

Like physical property, even intellectual property can be infringed upon. Although legal protection for IP is available round the world in the varying degree, still companies should remain vigilant about conserving their IP. Conserving includes both protecting IP from rivals as well as ensuring that benefits from IP are able to sustain for longer period of time. A conscious decision needs to be made for fixing the desirable level of IP protection. Local IP regulations and cost-benefit analysis should be taken into account before initiating legal action against the infringing party.

To sum up, for effective IP management in the organization, a right mix of all 5Cs is required. First of all although presented in an order, there is no need to undertake these five activities in the mentioned order sequentially. Rather, all these 5Cs are mutually supportive, and are to be managed simultaneously for improving IP management in the organization. Secondly, activities across all 5Cs should be coordinated and should perform as complements to one another. With the growth of the knowledge economy, attention towards IP management is further expected to increase. As technologies get mature and there is little in terms of technology differentiation across the organizations, IP management will become an important determinant of the competitive advantage. Firms should ensure that IP management and organization is in place for survival and success in the future competitive landscape.

9.5 SUMMARY

IP management deals with the acquisition, exploitation, and protection of intellectual property in an organization. Due to increased importance of IP in the business, IP management is also catching attention of the business managers. There are a number IP management activities such as undertaking IP Intelligence, acquisition of IP, managing IP Portfolio, supporting deployment IP in products and services, commercialization of IP, protecting IP, preparation and implementation of IP policy and carrying out IP audits. IP management has been summed up using 5Cs namely, carving, creating, commercializing, capturing and conserving.

CASE STUDY—IP MANAGEMENT AT IITD AND IITB

Indian Institute of Technology Delhi (IITD) and India Institute of Technology Bombay (IITB) are the premiere technology institutes of India actively engaged in the education and research activities. For managing IP activities IITD and IITB have come up with Foundation for Innovation and Technology Transfer (FITT) and Industrial Research and Consultancy Center (IRCC) respectively. IP management activities at IITD and IITB are further explained in this case.

FITT AT INDIAN INSTITUTE OF TECHNOLOGY DELHI

Established in 1992 as a registered society, FITT is the industrial interface of IITD. The mission of FITT is to be an effective interface with the industry to foster, promote and sustain commercialization of science and technology in the Institute for mutual benefits. Since its inception, FITT has been making efforts for maintaining the interface between the Institute and the industry and has been devising innovative ways to create partnerships and linkages with business and community to enable knowledge transfer for common good. Role of FITT is in the areas of fostering technology development, technical consultancy, collaborative R&D, professional HR development programmes, industry-site visits, event participation, corporate membership, etc. Key agenda of the foundation is to showcase and transfer the

Institute "intellectual ware" to industry and also inject industrial relevance in teaching and research at IITD.

IITD considers scientific and technological advancement as an important catalytic factor in industrial development and economic progress. The Institute encourages protection of intellectual assets to foster innovation and create opportunities for wealth creation. FITT facilitates and manages the Institute IPR activities. It receives information, carries out analysis and due diligence and processes for registration and maintenance of IP. Bulk of actual filings, though are outsourced.

Source: Adapted from www.fitt-iitd.org

IRCC AT INDIAN INSTITUTE OF TECHNOLOGY BOMBAY

IIT Bombay defines its vision as 'to be the fountainhead of new ideas and of innovators in technology and science' and its mission statement is 'to create an ambience in which new ideas, research and scholarship flourish and from which the leaders and innovators of tomorrow emerge'. For following this vision and mission, IITB has taken the initiative to promote innovations and to facilitate protection of IP generated at IITB. IRCC at IITB provides guidance, support and resources to all IITB personnel and facilitates protection and deployment of intellectual property. In achieving this goal, IRCC creates awareness of the importance and role of IP Rights, implements the IP policy, ensures transparency and fairness of the IP policy to encourage compliance, solicits feedback regarding the fulfillment of the IP policy and periodically reviews the policy to improve upon any shortcomings, strengthens the infrastructure and resources for protection and exploitation. IRCC conducts workshops to enhance awareness on issues, such as ownership, confidentiality, disclosure, patentability, technology transfer, revenue sharing, and conflict of interest. IRCC also provides templates and guidelines for the contracts, agreements and MOUs governing the effective exploitation of the IP produced by IITB. All such agreements and matters relating to confidentiality, infringements, damages, liabilities and compliance are administered by IRCC.

Source: Adapted from www.ircc.iitb.ac.in

Issues for Discussion

1. Discuss the purpose for creation of FITT and IRCC.
2. What type of role is being played by FITT and IRCC for promoting IP at IITD and IITB, respectively?
3. Comment on the alternatives available for IITD and IITB for exploiting maximum value from their IP assets.

Discussion Questions

1. Why there is a need to manage intellectual property in business?
2. Discuss in detail the process of undertaking IP intelligence.

3. Why there is a need for protecting IP of an organization?
4. What are the methods for commercializing IP?
5. What is IP policy? Explain the purpose of having IP policy in the organization.
6. Differentiate between 'Licensing out' and 'Cross-licensing'.
7. Write short note on the following:
   (a) IP Audit
   (b) IP Intelligence
   (c) IP Policy
8. "Creating IP is important, capturing value of IP is still more important". Comment on the statement.

Objective Type Questions

Tick the right answer in given multiple-choice questions:

1. Consideration for licensing in an IP is termed as
   (a) Interest (b) Royalty (c) Bonus (d) Dividend
2. A firm licensing in an IP is called
   (a) Licensor (b) Licensee (c) Buyer (d) None of these
3. A firm licensing out an IP is called
   (a) Licensor (b) Licensee (c) Seller (d) None of these
4. Which of the following is not an environmental mapping process
   (a) Scanning (b) Measuring (c) Monitoring (d) Assessing
5. IP assets cannot lose their value by
   (a) Obsolescence (b) Licensing (c) Infringement (d) None of these
6. Which one of the following is not an external source of acquiring IP
   (a) Research Consortium (b) Joint venture (c) Universities
   (d) None of these
7. Which of the following is not a reason being licensing out an IP
   (a) Earning royalty (b) Freedom to operate
   (c) Developing industry standard (d) None of these
8. Licensing out an IP may lead to
   (a) Decreased royalties (b) Competition in market place
   (c) Infringements (d) None of these
9. Which one of the following is not a technology forecasting technique
   (a) S-curve approach (b) Morphological Analysis (c) Simulation
   (d) Licensing
10. Which of the following is not an IP management activity
   (a) Audit (b) IP Commercialization (c) Protection (d) Marketing

Mark TRUE or FALSE against given statements:

1. Cross-licensing is done to avoid mutual IP litigations. (True/False)
2. Value of IP can be lost on account of infringement. (True/False)
3. In-house R&D is the only source for IP acquisition. (True/False)
4. Royalties on an IP are paid by the licensor. (True/False)
5. Cross licensing is not prevalent in semiconductor industry. (True/False)

References

Bhatia, V. and Carey, G. (2007), Patenting for profits, *MIT Sloan Management Review*, Summer, pp. 15–16.

Lichtenthaler, U. (2007), The drivers of technology licensing: An industry comparison, *California Management Review*, Volume 49, No. 4, pp. 67–89.

Nevens, T.M., Summe, G.L. and Uttal, B. (1990), Commercializing technology: What best companies do, *Harvard Business Review*, May–June, pp. 154–162.

Pisano, G.P. and Teece, D.T. (2007), How to capture value from innovation: shaping intellectual property and industry architecture, *California Management Review*, Volume 50, No. 1, pp. 278–296.

Reitzig, M. (2007), How executives can enhance IP strategy and performance, *MIT Sloan Management Review*, Fall, pp. 37–43.

CHAPTER 10

Emerging Issues in IPR

Intellectual Property Rights have hogged the limelight since the signing up of agreement on TRIPS in 1995. IPRs are the creation of the human mind and the assets of the emerging knowledge economy. Owing to the dynamics of the knowledge economy, rapid pace of technological change and IPRs being adopted worldwide within the ambit of the standard procedures prescribed by TRIPS, the field of intellectual property is full of issues and contentions. The present flux in the field is mainly caused by a number of emerging issues and no discussion on IPR can be complete without reference to these issues. These issues range from sectors like agriculture and public health to the challenges posed by the fast paced technological changes especially in the field of internet. Major issues emerging on the horizons of intellectual property are being discussed as follows:

- Public Health and TRIPS
- Traditional Knowledge and Bio-piracy
- Trade marks vs. Geographical Indications
- Open Source Movement
- Internet and IPRs
- Patent Sharks
- Concentration of IP
- Protection of plant varieties and farmers' Rights

10.1 TRIPS AND PUBLIC HEALTH

One area where agreement on TRIPS has got maximum impact is public health. Patents in medicine can result in higher prices that are unaffordable for the masses in the developing nations. No doubt that patent protection leads to the development of new and better products by the organizations undertaking successful R&D, but at the same time it also pushes up the prices. Price of the medicine comes down with the increase in the competition as the medicine moves to the generic category (off-patent). Increased medicine prices may spell havoc for the poor in the developing countries as inability to purchase the costly medicine may lead to a life and death situation. Developing countries like India and Brazil have been taking up this issue at WTO with the active support of African countries. Although, Article 31 of agreement on TRIPS has got the provision of compulsory licensing, still the patent regime remains at the loggerheads with the policy of public health.

Another related issue in this regard is that of 'Parallel Imports'. Parallel import is the process of importing lawfully manufactured and marketed products from another country without the consent of the patent holder. By permitting parallel imports, the countries are able to identify the lowest prices for the lawfully marketed medicines worldwide and undertake imports. Issue of contention is that whether such imports can be undertaken without the consent of the patent holder.

Major criticism of agreement on TRIPS in this regard comes from the availability, accessibility and affordability of the medicines. As patients of HIV/AIDS continue to grow in India, there is a pertinent need for reducing the prices of the medicine. This reduction is possible if highly production-efficient pharmaceutical industry in India is not unduly constrained by the new patent regime. In fact, the prices of HIV/AIDS medicine in India are lower at least five to six times than that of the original products being sold in USA and UK. But the same story is not replicated everywhere, and the poor in the other developing countries, especially the African countries, still find life saving drugs out of their reach.

10.2 TRADITIONAL KNOWLEDGE AND BIO-PIRACY

Bio-piracy can be defined as the hijacking of knowledge and genetic resources belonging to farming and indigenous communities by the parties seeking exclusive control over these resources through obtaining intellectual property, such as patents. Bio-piracy can be primarily attributed to inefficient IP systems that are not able to identify the origin of a claim for the intellectual property in the traditional knowledge of a community. Inefficiency of the IP systems is usually reflected by the oversight of the patent examiners to these sources of knowledge. At times, the traditional knowledge, though in written form, is not available to the patent examiners but in majority of the cases reported under bio-piracy such knowledge is un-written but widespread as the community knowledge.

There is vast amount of traditional knowledge that is passed on to one generation to the other in the unwritten form such as the medicinal properties of *turmeric*, *neem* and *aanwla* are communicated from one generation to another in India. This traditional knowledge is usually not available in the written form, and if even if written records and documents are available, these are not digitized. On account of the absence of digitized traditional knowledge the patent examiners are not able to take into account the fact that the basic requirement of novelty in case of grant of patents stand violated. Government of India has made an effort to digitize the traditional knowledge, but given the vastness and diversity of the country, digitization of traditional knowledge still remains an elusive goal. Traditional Knowledge Digital Library (TKDL) has been created and efforts are being made to digitize the knowledge from Ayurveda (a traditional Indian medicine system). TKDL is expected to provide legitimacy to the existing traditional knowledge and refrain the related attempts of bio-piracy.

10.3 TRADE MARKS vs. GEOGRAPHICAL INDICATIONS

TRIPS aims at providing protection to the specialties of a region under 'Geographical Indications'. This agreement also provides international protection to Geographical Indications with higher protection in case of wines and spirits (under article 23 of agreement on TRIPS). But the controversy between the European Union and United States of America refuses to settle down. United States treats registered trade marks at the marks superior to Geographical Indications, and has refused to sign the Lisbon agreement that establishes superiority of Geographical Indications over the trade marks. Owing to the commercial interest of the parties advocating and opposing the superiority of Geographical Indications over trade marks, the solution is in sight. Simultaneously, the voices of extending Article 23 to goods other than wine and spirits are also getting louder.

10.4 OPEN SOURCE MOVEMENT

Open source refers to the arrangement in the software development to make available the source code of the computer program in the public domain so that other developers can build upon the code base. Open source licensing arrangements provide the liberty to the developers to use open source code and develop on it as long as they are not trying to appropriate the previously used code. Known examples of open source code include Linux and Apache. Traditionally, software developers have tried to conceal the source code and have even made attempts to seek legal protection for this purpose. Philosophy of open source code works in the opposite manner and the developers make available the source code for everyone to use. Open source ushers in the creation of a commonly shared base of technology that is useful for everyone. Open source code movement has thrown considerable challenges to the firms, like Microsoft and Sun who have sought protection to their operating systems by concealing the source code.

10.5 INTERNET AND IPRS

With the expansion of internet its ability to disseminate information, content and knowledge has also multiplied. Rapid changes in the internet technologies have certainly outpaced the legislation regulating internet as well as intellectual property regime. On account of the gap between the scope of intellectual property regulations and advances in the technology, a number of issues have come up. Out of these issues, internet domain names and copyrights have been much prominent. For this reason, these two issues are being discussed as follows:

10.5.1 Internet Domain Name

Internet domain name is basically the address of a website. Website owners want to have a name that is easy to remember and use so that to have maximum hits. In case of business organizations most of the times, trade marks are used as the internet domain names. Use of trade marks as internet domain name helps surfers to identify the website of company and navigate. For example, amazon.com uses the trade mark of Amazon. Off late, internet domain names have led to a number of disputes arising from the practice of cyber squatting. Cyber squatting is the practice of pre-emptive registration of trade marks by third parties as domain names. First-come first serve nature of the domain name registration system has led to the squatting of internet domain names related to trade marks, celebrities and business houses. Due to simplicity of the domain name registration system, cyber squatters manage to get the internet domain names for a nominal amount and use this registration for making a handsome profit by selling these domain names to the persons and organizations. Although, WIPO has started initiatives in collaboration with the concerned parties in the internet domain registration system, yet avoiding pre-emptive owning of domain names belonging to others remains a cause for dispute.

10.5.2 Copyright and Internet

Any type of copying technology has been a threat to the copyright owners. Widespread photo-copiers have always dealt a blow to the profits of the publishers and book sellers. Photocopiers were able to affect the profit figures of the copyright holders, but did not threaten their fundamental business model primarily on two counts—firstly the process of photocopying carried a cost component, and secondly the quality of copied material was quite inferior as compared to the original product. But with the advent of digital technology and internet there is an imminent threat to the fundamental business models of the copyright holders, because using digital technology perfect replicas can be generated without any incremental cost and further, these can be distributed using internet with very little effort and cost. Any music CD copied into mp3 format can be distributed and downloaded in minutes at very nominal cost. One can get mp3 versions of newly released music albums on internet free of cost and even the motion pictures are meeting the same fate. Using Bluetooth, attachment applications and MMS songs and video clips can be forwarded without substantial cost. Although, the companies engaged in the music industry are coming up with products to tackle this problem (such as launch of CDs by Sony that cannot be run on computers yet in the absence of the law enforcement unauthorized copying and distribution remains a contentious issue.

10.5.3 Software Piracy

Globerman (1998) has defined software policy as unauthorized duplication, distribution, and downloading of computer programs and applications. Software piracy has emerged as a global problems and the deep embedded in the human behaviour as well as the weakness of IP enforcement mechanism in place. Business Software Alliance (BSA) conducts studies on the prevalence of software piracy every year. As per the figures of BSA 2010 study, the highest piracy rate was found in Zimbabwe and Georgia with the figures of 92 percent and 91 percent respectively. China was stated to have piracy rate of 77 percent, while India was reported to have piracy rate of 63 percent. Going by the commercial value of pirated software, United States was reported to be at the top with the figures of 9773 million dollars in 2011. Estimates for China, Russia, and India stood at 8902 million dollars, 3227 million dollars and 2930 million dollars respectively. BSA has suggested a number of measures for reducing the software piracy and these include:

- Increasing public awareness about the issue
- Effective legal enforcement for copyright protection
- Carving out strong and functional IPR enforcement under WTO

10.6 PATENT SHARKS

Henkel and Reitzig (2008) have coined the term 'Patent Sharks' for the firms that prefer to maintain hidden intellectual property rights and threaten to sue when their rights are inadvertently infringed. These firms behave like sharks that remain under water and are known for their sudden and sharp attacks. Patent sharks usually operate in the sectors, such as telecommunications, mobile communications and computing. Most of the times these sharks are not manufacturing products based on their IP and purchase these IP from other firms at cheaper rates. To begin with patent sharks remain hidden and do not act instantaneously when their rights are infringed rather wait for an opportune time. This opportune time is usually marked by the success of the products (products embedded with the IP belonging to patent sharks) of the target. As soon as the opportunity matures these sharks strike and threaten other firms (the ones who have unknowingly infringed IP of sharks) with legal suits. Normally, patent sharks go for out of court settlements, and are able to make a fortune out of such deals. Patent sharks have been active in USA and Europe and with passage of time are likely to emerge in the developing countries like India. There is an urgent need for revising the existing laws so that patent sharks can be curbed.

10.7 CONCENTRATION OF IP

From the available data it seems that patent filings and grants are concentrated to only handful nations in the world. Consider the following data reflected in the World Intellectual Property Indicators 2009 (a publication of WIPO):

- Out of total 6.3 million patents in force worldwide approximately 47 percent are owned by the residents of USA and Japan.
- In 2007, about 59.2 percent of total patent filings came from China, Japan and United States.
- Residents of Japan, Republic of Korea and USA received 63.4 percent of the total patents granted worldwide in 2007.
- Trend of seeking protection of intellectual property rights outside the domestic markets is picking up with non-residents receiving 43.9 percent of total patent grants in 2007.

There are a few trends that are reflected from the facts given ahead. First of all there is concentration of worldwide patent filing as well as grants with countries such as USA, Japan, China and Republic of Korea. This concentration should not come as surprise as these four are the leading countries sin terms of ratio of expenditure on R&D to GDP. Another important trend to be noticed is that patent applicants are moving out of their domestic markets and seeking protection in the foreign markets. This is the indication of globalization of the intellectual property regime, whereby the inventors are hopeful of exploiting their IPs internationally. For this very reason applications under Patent Cooperation Treaty (PCT) are going up.

10.8 PROTECTION OF PLANT VARIETIES AND FARMERS' RIGHTS

Process of plant breeding is long and expensive. New varieties are expected to have significant impact on the income of the farmers and are the harbingers of overall economic development. Paragraph 3 of Article 27 of agreement on TRIPS provides that the member countries may exclude from the patentability the plants and animals other than micro-organisms, and essentially biological processes for the production of plants or animals other than non-biological and microbiological processes. However, members shall provide for the protection of plant varieties either by patents or by an effective *sui generis* system or by any combination thereof. Sui generis system means a system that is of its own kind. Sui generis system followed in India for the protection of plant varieties has been provided by 'The Protection of Plant Varieties and Farmers' Rights (PPV & FR) Act 2001'. Detailed discussion on PPV & FR Act has been presented in Annexure.

10.9 SUMMARY

Intellectual property rights have caught the attention of the academicians and business organizations after implementation of the agreement on TRIPS. Being in the preliminary evolution stage a number of issues related to intellectual property rights have emerged. This chapter presents various emerging issues in the field of intellectual property rights. Issues such as TRIPS and public health, open source movement, impact of internet, etc. have been discussed in this chapter. Towards the end of the chapter, a brief discussion on Protection of Plant Varieties and Farmers' Rights has been presented.

Annexure

PPV & FR was enacted on 30 October 2001 in India. This act provides for the establishment of an effective system for protection of plant varieties, the rights of farmers and plant breeders and to encourage the development of new varieties of plants. Major aims of PPV & FR act have been listed as follows:

- To recognize and protect the rights of the farmers in respect of their contribution made at any time in conserving, improving and making available plant genetic resources for the development of new plant varieties
- To protect plant breeders' rights to stimulate investment for research and development, both in the public and private sector, for the development of new plant varieties; for accelerated agricultural development in the country
- To facilitate the growth of the seed industry in the country which will ensure the availability of high quality seeds and planting material to the farmers by providing protection to new plant varieties and farmers' rights

Section 2(l) of the Act defines 'farmer' as any person who cultivates crops by cultivating the land himself or cultivates crops by directly supervising the cultivation or land through any other person or conserves and preserves with any other person any wild species or traditional varieties or adds value to such wild species of traditional variety through selection and identification of their useful properties.

Chapter VI Section 39(1) of the Act provides the farmers' right as under:

- Farmer who has bred or developed a new variety shall be entitled for registration and other protection under PPV & FR Act, 2001 in the same manner as a breeder of a variety.

- Farmer who is engaged in the conservation of genetic resources of land races and wild relatives of economic plants and their improvement through selection and preservation shall be entitled in the prescribed manner for recognition and reward from the Gene Fund provided that material so selected and preserved has been used as donors of genes in varieties registered under this act.
- Farmer shall be entitle to save, use, sow, re-sow, exchange and share or sell his farm produce including seed of a variety protected under this act in the same manner as he was entitled before the coming into force of this act provided that the farmer shall not be entitled to sell branded seed of a variety protected under this act.

Under this act 'Protection of Plant Varieties and Farmers' Rights Authority' has been set up. Registration of new varieties can be done with:

Registrar,
Protection of Plant Varieties and Farmers' Rights Authority,
NASC Complex, DPS Marg,
Opposite Todapur, New Delhi-110012

Application to the registrar can be made of a variety of such genera and species as specified by Government of India in the official gazette from time to time. Application for the registration of extant variety and farmers' variety can also be made under this Act. For registration of new variety under PPV & FR, the following criteria have been specified:

- Novelty
- Distinct
- Uniform
- Stable

1. **Novelty:** A variety will be novel, if, at the date of filing of the application for registration for protection, the propagating or harvested material of such variety has not been sold or otherwise disposed of by or with the consent of its breeder or his successor for the purposes of exploitation of such variety in India, earlier than one year; or outside India, in the case of trees or vines earlier than six years, or in any other case, earlier than four years before the date of filing such application.
2. **Distinct:** The variety will be treated as distinct if it is clearly distinguishable by at least one essential characteristic from any other variety whose existence is a matter of common knowledge in any country at the time of filing of the application.
3. **Uniform:** The variety will be treated as uniform if subject to the variation that may be expected from the particular features of its propagation is sufficiently uniform in its essential characteristics.

4. **Stable:** This condition requires that essential characteristics of the variety remain unchanged after repeated propagation or, in the case of a particular cycle of propagation, at the end of each such cycle.

Duration of protection of the registered varieties is given below:

For trees and vines: 18 years
For other crops: 15 years
For extant varieties: 15 years

Protection period will start from the date of notification of that variety by the Government of India under section 5 of Seeds Act, 1966.

Discussion Questions

1. Define Bio-piracy. Discuss the loopholes in the patent regime paving way for 'Bio-piracy'.
2. Discuss in detail the impact of internet on intellectual property rights.
3. What are the patent sharks? How do these patent sharks operate?
4. What do you understand by 'Cyber squatting'?
5. Discuss in detail the major aims of PPV & FR Act.
6. Elaborate the criteria for the registration of a plant variety under PPV & FR.
7. Write short note on the following:
   (a) Parallel Imports
   (b) Patent Sharks
   (c) Copyright and Internet
8. "Internet has thrown a number of challenges to the IPR regime". Comment on the statement.

Objective Type Questions

Tick the right answer in given multiple-choice questions:

1. The Registry of PPV & FR authority in India is at
   (a) New Delhi (b) Kolkata (c) Chennai (d) Mumbai
2. Importing an article from a foreign country without the permission of patent holder is called
   (a) Compulsory licensing (b) Deemed import (c) Parallel imports
   (d) None of these
3. Article 31 of TRIPS deals with
   (a) Cross licensing (b) Parallel imports (c) Compulsory licensing
   (d) None of these

4. Which of the following country has not signed Lisbon Agreement
   (a) India (b) UK (c) France (d) USA
5. Pre-emptive registration of trade marks by the third party as internet domain name is called
   (a) Hacking (b) Cyber squatting (c) Phishing (d) Cyber stalking
6. Which of the following follows open source movement
   (a) Microsoft (b) Linux (c) Sun Microsystems (d) None of these
7. Off-patent medicines are also termed as
   (a) Specialty medicines (b) Generic (c) Life saving drugs
   (d) None of these
8. PPV & FR Act came into being in
   (a) 1995 (b) 1997 (c) 1999 (d) 2001
9. Which one of the following is not a part of criteria followed for the registration of plant varieties under PPV & FR Act
   (a) Novelty (b) Uniformity (c) Stability (d) Industrial Use
10. Duration of protection for varieties of trees under PPV & FR Act is
    (a) 10 years (b) 14 years (c) 18 years (d) 20 years

Mark TRUE or FALSE against given statements:

1. Article 23 of TRIPS provides special protection to spirits and wines. (True/False)
2. India follows sui generis system for the protection of plant varieties. (True/False)
3. USA is not signatory to Lisbon Agreement. (True/False)
4. Apache is part of open source movement. (True/False)
5. TKDL can help controlling bio-pircay. (True/False)

References

Globerman, S. (1988), Addressing international product piracy, *Journal of International Business Studies*, 19(3), pp. 175–186.

Henkel, J. and Reitzig, M. (2008), Patent Sharks, *Harvard Business Review*, June, pp. 129–133.

World Intellectual Property Indicators (2009), A Publication of WIPO.

Websites

www.bsa.org Eighth Annual BSA Global Software 2010 Piracy Study

www.wto.org

www.wipo.int

Case Studies

CASE STUDY 1

Research and Development in India

Research and Development (R&D) has been widely recognized as the engine of economic development and growth. R&D initiatives are aimed at achieving a number of objectives, such as creation of new product, improving an existing product and lowering the cost by means of changes in product and process design. R&D expenditure is motivated by monetary as well as non-monetary benefits arising from R&D output. In the contemporary economies, conscious efforts are made for improving R&D investments and outcomes.

R&D SCENARIO IN INDIA—AN OVERVIEW

R&D expenditure of India from 1995–1996 to 2007–2008 has been presented in Table CS 1.1. It can be seen from the table that for the year 2007–2008, R&D expenditure stood at ₹377777.90 crores. This figure turns out to be less than one percent of Indian GDP.

Table CS 1.1 R&D Expenses in India (1995–1996 to 2007–2008)

Year	*R&D Expenses (₹ Crores)*	*GDP (₹ Crores)*	*R&D as Percentage of GDP*
1995–1996	7483.88	1083289	0.69
1996–1997	8913.61	1260710	0.71
1997–1998	10611.34	1401934	0.76
1998–1999	12473.17	1616082	0.77
1999–2000	14397.60	1786526	0.81
2000–2001	16198.80	1925017	0.84
2001–2002	17038.15	2097726	0.81
2002–2003	18088.16	2261415	0.80
2003–2004	20086.34	2538171	0.79
2004–2005	24117.24	2877706	0.84
2005–2006	28776.65	3275670	0.88
2006–2007	32941.64	3790063	0.88
2007–2008	37777.90	4283000	0.89
CAGR	14.44	12.14	2.14

Source: Department of Science and Technology, Economic Survey (Various Issues), Authors' calculations.

Further, it can be seen from the table that Compound Annual Growth Rate (CAGR) for R&D expenditure in India has just managed to outpace the growth rate of GDP for the time period shown in the table. Available data indicate that as percentage of GDP, R&D expenditure in India has almost stagnated during the last 10 years of the time period shown in Table CS 1.1.

Role of Public Sector in Indian R&D

Table CS 1.2 presents sector-wise distribution of R&D expenditure in India from 2001–2002 to 2007–2008. It can be seen from the table that almost two-third of R&D expenditure for the year 2007–2008 came from Centre and State Governments, indicating their dominant contribution in the total R&D expenditure. Figures indicate gradual increase in the contribution by the private sector. Contribution of private sector in total R&D expenditure was about 19 percent in 2001–2002. Over a period of six years, this contribution was touching 30 percent. On the other hand, contribution of R&D expenditure from higher education has remained steady at about 4.5 percent level. Overall, it can be deduced that the contribution of private expenditure is on the rise in India, but the public sector is expected to retain its dominant position in the times to come.

Table CS 1.2 Sectoral Distribution of R&D Expenses (₹ Crores) in India (2001–2002 to 2007–2008)

Year	*Centre and State Government*	*Private Sector*	*Higher Education*	*Total*
2001–2002	13030.96 (76.48)	3239.69 (19.01)	714.80 (4.20)	17038.15 (100.00)
2002–2003	13839.32 (76.51)	3498.30 (19.34)	750.54 (4.15)	18088.16 (100.00)
2003–2004	14724.47 (73.31)	4471.27 (22.26)	890.60 (4.43)	20086.34 (100.00)
2004–2005	17021.48 (70.58)	6038.96 (25.04)	1056.80 (4.38)	24117.24 (100.00)
2005–2006	20078.43 (69.77)	7444.21 (25.87)	1254.01 (4.36)	28776.65 (100.00)
2006–2007	22370.31 (67.91)	9128.09 (27.71)	1443.24 (4.38)	32941.64 (100.00)
2007–2008	24924.01 (65.98)	11192.86 (29.63)	1661.03 (4.40)	37777.90 (100.00)

Source: Department of Science and Technology, Authors' calculations.

Public spending on R&D is a major contributor to the overall R&D spending of the economies worldwide. Public sector mainly includes R&D

expenses by government and higher education sector. According to World Intellectual Property Report 2011, public sector in the high-income countries spends 20 to 45 percent of total R&D expenditure. Moreover, the contribution of the public sector in the basic research in these countries is more than 75 percent, as the public sector R&D investment largely focuses on the basic research. Basic research can be defined as the experimental/theoretical work with the aim of acquiring new knowledge without specific use or application in sight. Recent trends indicate that the private sector, especially the Multinational Corporations (MNCs) are more interested in applied research such as product development and process improvement. On account of decreasing R&D expenditure on the basic research by the private sector, the onus of investing in the basic research, on the part of the public sector, can be expected to increase. Higher education institutes along with the public research agencies are expected to lead the new knowledge creation and dissemination in the economy. In the contemporary knowledge era, the importance of such institutions and agencies is bound to increase.

Major scientific agencies engaged in Research and Development in India are listed as follows:

1. Council for Scientific and Industrial Research (CSIR)
2. Defence Research and Development Organization (DRDO)
3. Indian Council of Agricultural Research (ICAR)
4. Indian Council of Medical Research (ICMR)
5. Department of Atomic Energy (DAE)
6. Department of Biotechnology (DBT)
7. Department of Science and Technology (DST)
8. Department of Space
9. Ministry of Communication and Information Technology
10. Ministry of New and Renewable Energy
11. Ministry of Ocean Development

These scientific agencies are expected to lead the knowledge creation and IP generation activities in the future. Council for Scientific and Industrial Research (CSIR) is the leading public sector research agency for IP generation in India. CSIR has proven to be the leading IP generator for the country. CSIR emerged as one of the top patent seekers at the global level in 2003. As per the available data for the year 2003, out of total 342 patents granted to Indian applicants by United Stated Patent and Trademark Office (USPTO), 133 patents were bagged by CSIR.

IP Generation

Table CS 1.3 shows patent applications filed in India from 2000–2001 to 2006–2007. Data clearly indicates the dominant position of Foreign Residents in context of patent filing in India.

Table CS 1.3 Applications for Patents Filed in India (2000–2001 to 2006–2007)

Year	*From India*	*From Foreign Residents Abroad*	*Total*
2000–2001	2179 (25.63)	6324 (74.37)	8503 (100.00)
2001–2002	2371 (22.38)	8221 (77.62)	10592 (100.00)
2002–2003	2693 (23.49)	8773 (76.51)	11466 (100.00)
2003–2004	3218 (25.51)	9395 (74.49)	12613 (100.00)
2004–2005	3630 (20.78)	13836 (79.22)	17466 (100.00)
2005–2006	4521 (18.45)	19984 (81.55)	24505 (100.00)
2006–2007	5314 (18.36)	23626 (81.64)	28940 (100.00)

Source: Annual Reports of the Controller General of Patents, Designs and Trade Marks.

Further, it can be noted that share of Foreign Residents for patent filing in India is increasing steadily. Share of patent filing by Foreign Residents in India has gone up from 74.37 percent in 2000–2001 to 81.64 percent in 2006–2007.

R&D expenditure as percentage of GDP of selected countries for the year 2005–2006 has been presented in Table CS 1.4. It can be seen from the table that Israel, Finland and Japan are leading countries in terms of R&D expenditure as percentage of GDP. R&D spending in China was found to be 1.42 percent of GDP, while for India the figure stood at 0.88 percent.

Major Challenges

Indian pursuit for making dominant presence at the global level will be rendered futile in event of inadequate generation and exploitation of Intellectual Property assets. Major issues and challenges in the Indian R&D sector have been listed as follows:

1. **Indian R&D expenditure levels are lagging as compared to leading countries at the global platform.**
2. **There is an urgent need to prop up R&D expenditure and IP generation in the higher education sector.**
3. **There is need for better IP management so that IP assets can be put through the phase of commercialization.**
4. **There is a need on part of private sector to boost R&D expenditure.**

Table CS 1.4 R&D Expenditure as Percentage of GDP (2006)

Country	*R&D Expenditure*
Israel	4.53
Finland	3.43
Japan	3.40
South Korea	3.23
United States of America	2.61
Germany	2.52
Denmark	2.44
France	2.12
Canada	1.97
United Kingdom	1.80
Australia	1.78
Netherlands	1.69
Czech Republic	1.54
China	1.42
Russia	1.08
India	0.88
Brazil	0.82

Source: World Development Indicators (Various Issues), World Bank

Discussion Questions

1. How do you evaluate the current R&D scenario in India?
2. What can be the drivers of R&D expenditure in any economy?
3. Discuss the importance of Public Sector R&D expenditure for IP generation, especially in context of developing countries.
4. Suggest the ways for tackling the challenges faced by India in R&D sector.

CASE STUDY 2

Apple versus Samsung Patent Dispute

Apple Inc. is a Cupertino, California based organization having leading position across many product categories, like handsets, audio devices, laptops, tablets, personal computers, software and electronic accessories. It has iconic products like Macintosh PCs, iMac, Macbook Air, Macbook Pro, iPad, iTunes, iPod and iPhone. Apple Inc. is leading IT company contending for leadership position; currently being second in terms of revenue after Samsung Electronics. The success of iPhone has made Apple the third largest mobile handset manufacturer. Samsung, a South Korean MNC is the market leader in mobile handsets followed by Nokia and Apple. Being close competitors, Apple and Samsung have been locked in series of court battle over allegations and counter-allegations of patent infringements.

THE BEGINNING

Samsung Electronics is an aggressive player in the consumer electronics category. In April 2011, Apple Inc. filed infringement law suit against its component supplier Samsung Electronics at a district court in California. This was the time when many of the Samsung Android based mobile models, like Galaxy, Epic and Nexus had done extensively well in terms of sales volume and profitability. Apple claimed that several of Samsung Android mobile and tablet models had infringed upon many of the Apple's patents, trade mark and style. As a retaliatory move, Samsung also filed cases of patent infringement against Apple in the same month in Japan, USA, UK, Germany and South Korea. Samsung also filed a case against Apple at ITC (International Trade Commission) at Washington DC. There were series of claims and counter-claims by both the parties in the different court filings. Apple was already having court dispute over patent infringement with Motorola. The high stakes in terms of revenue and profitability due to growing demand in consumer electronics, particularly in the mobile handset category had further fuelled these patent wars.

PATENT WAR IN COURTROOMS

There were more than fifty cases going on between Apple Inc. and Samsung Electronics in about ten countries. In each of these cases there were charges of patent and trade mark infringement; including making the product indistinguishable to the customer due to the product similarities. For example, in one of the law suits filed by Apple Inc., it claimed that Samsung's Galaxy S i9000 was similar to Apple's iPhone 3GS, especially in terms of packaging. The patent infringements claims ran into billions of dollars including request for injunction from the trial court. In some of the cases during the course of the hearing the devices/model, regarding which the case was filed, were discontinued by the either party leading to new dimension to the pending court cases.

On 24 August 2012, the California district court found Samsung guilty of Apple patent infringements and fined Samsung $1.05 billion in damages. However, the injunction petition of Apple Inc. asking for stopping sales of specific Samsung products in USA accused of violating Apple patent was turned down by the court. Samsung filed request in a San Jose court on 21 September 2012 for retrial of the case citing limitations during the past hearing at California district court. It was accepted for retrial.

Meanwhile in a counter-offensive Samsung Electronics filed cases in South Korea, Germany, Japan, Italy, France, USA, Australia and UK against Apple Inc. for patent violation. The final judgment by three judge bench at Seoul, South Korea in August 2012 found both, Samsung and Apple, guilty of patent violations of each other and ordered small damages. It also ordered ban on sales of specific product models for both the parties. This ban on sales of specific product models had little impact as most of them were older models. The Japanese court, in its final judgment, in August 2012 did not find any of Apple's claims of patent violation against Samsung to be true. It ordered Apple to reimburse all the legal cost incurred by Samsung in the Japanese court. In German courts Apple got injunction against sale of Samsung specific product models. The court found that Samsung was guilty of certain patent infringements that were in the name of Apple Inc. In courts of Germany, Italy, France, Australia and UK there was a mixed verdict for both the parties viz. Samsung Electronics and Apple Inc. in terms of monetary damages and injunction.

Update

The legal battle between these two big consumer electronics players viz. Samsung and Apple over patent infringement continues. In the latest development, on 1 March 2013, the California district court reduced the monetary damages to Samsung from $1.05 billion to $598.9 million. This 43 percent reduction was seen as big relief for Samsung and which may further lead to a final settlement between the two competitors.

Implications

The $ 1.05 billion damages slapped against many of Samsung Android mobile and tablet models; which was later reduced by the jury; will have cascading effect on pricing; innovation and consumer electronics industry. These patent disputes are going to get more complex with other intellectual properties like trade mark, design and style infringements issues being brought before the jury. This was witnessed during the case proceedings of Apple versus Samsung patent dispute.

The California court ruling may also impact usage of Google's Android as operating system in different devices inter alia mobile handsets and tablets. The upcoming innovation and product launches by different organizations may try to avoid Apple-Samsung type of technological overlap disputes. Many of the telecom players including Samsung, Nokia and Motorola have agreement for payment of license fee for patent usage with the patent holder of particular technologies.

Majority of the innovations (more than 98%) today are incremental innovations. In such a scenario, chances of technology overlap and evergreening trends are higher. The consumer electronics majors, like Samsung Electronics, Nokia, Apple Inc., Research in Motion (RIM), etc. have filed thousands of patents to protect design and functionality of their equipment. Many of them are being renewed by their original patent holders just before its expiry by undertaking incremental innovations on that product; leaving fewer opportunities for other players to enter into that particular domain; unless the other player comes up with a radical innovation. This evergreening phenomenon negatively impacts the culture of creativity and innovation in a country. The Indian patent laws do not allow for evergreening of patent. The organizations have to ensure that due diligence is followed in licensing permissions and patent transfer & assignments, wherever necessary, in order to avoid lengthy and costly litigation process.

Discussion Questions

1. What are the key learnings from above Apple–Samsung patent dispute case?
2. What would have been the impact in case Samsung products were banned in USA as demanded by Apple in injunction proceedings?
3. Suggest the ways for tackling the challenges of evergreening of patents.
4. What may be the possible reasons of different court verdicts in different countries in the Apple–Samsung patent dispute case?

References

Apple–Samsung Ruling: Emerging Markets View (2012), *Emerging Markets Monitor, Business Monitor International*, Volume 18, No. 22, September, pp. 1–4.

Apple Inc. versus Samsung Electronics Co., Ltd.; Wikipedia; Available at http://en.wikipedia.org/wiki/Apple_Inc._v._Samsung_Electronics_Co.,_Ltd.

Cusumano, Michael A. (2013), Technology Strategy and Management: The Apple–Samsung Lawsuits, Communications of the ACM, January, Volume 55, No. 1, pp. 28–31.

Sherr, Ian (2013), U.S. Judge Reduces Apple's Patent Award in Samsung Case , The Wall Street Journal, Friday, March 1; Available at http://online.wsj.com/article/SB10001424127887323478304578334540541100744.html

Vascellaro, Jessica E. (2012), Apple Wins Big in Patent Case, The Wall Street Journal, Saturday, August 25; Available at http://online.wsj.com/article/SB10000872396390444358404577609810658082898.html

Websites

http://www.samsung.com/in/

http://www.apple.com/in/

Index